THE INNER LIFE

THE
INNER LIFE

Hazrat Inayat Khan

Shambhala

BOSTON & LONDON
1997

Shambhala Publications, Inc.
Horticultural Hall
300 Massachusetts Avenue
Boston, MA 02115
http://www.shambhala.com

© 1997 by International Headquarters of the Sufi Movement

9 8 7 6 5 4 3 2

Printed in the United States of America

⊗ This edition is printed on acid-free paper that meets the
American National Standards Institute z39.48 Standard.

Distributed in the United States by Random House, Inc., and in
Canada by Random House of Canada Ltd

Library of Congress Cataloging-in-Publication Data
Khan, Hazrat Inayat.
The inner life/Hazrat Inayat Khan.—1st ed.
p. cm.
Includes bibliographical references and index.
ISBN 1-57062-209-4 (alk. paper)
1. Sufism. I. Title.
BP189.K474   1997   96-27145
297'.4—dc20   CIP

Contents

Foreword

THIS BOOK BRINGS TOGETHER some teachings on the mystical path by one of the most extraordinary personalities of the present time: Pir-o-Murshid Hazrat Inayat Khan. Hazrat Inayat Khan was a famous Indian musician and illuminated mystic who went to the Western world to give an answer to its deepest needs in his Sufi message.

Looking at his early life, it is striking how everything—his background, his family, his musical career, his spiritual search, and his life experiences—prepared him for his great mission of bringing the Sufi message to the Western world.[1]

He was born on 5 July 1882 in Baroda, India. Baroda was a progressive state. Its maharaja saw as ideal that India and the West would learn from each other: Europe and America would be inspired by Indian spirituality and India would learn technology and economic progress from the West.

Everyone in Inayat Khan's family was very gifted. His grandfather, Maula Bakhsh, was a great musician who developed a musical notation system that brought together the music of northern and southern India. He also studied Western music and founded a music academy in Baroda, the Gayanshala. Inayat Khan's father, Rahmat Khan, was also an accomplished musician and dhrupad singer. Many musicians, poets, and philosophers, both Muslim and Hindu, met in Maula Bakhsh's house. Thus, Inayat Khan grew up in an atmosphere that was inspiring, universal, and open to all, beyond distinctions and differences. And although his family had a Muslim background, he was sent to a Hindu school. Thus, from the beginning he was open to all religions.

A very close relationship developed between Inayat Khan and his grandfather. When he was a boy he used to spend mornings with him practicing music and singing. In this way he developed his talent and became a great musician. While he was still very young he was invited to sing at the courts of different maharajas. He reached the culmination of his career in Hyderabad, where the nizam was open to music and spirituality and was deeply impressed by Inayat. The nizam felt that there was great depth behind his music. He gave him the name Tansen, after the famous singer at the court of King Akbar.

Hazrat Inayat Khan's musical proficiency was extraordinary. But his music was devotional and meditative. He sang to God in love and devotion, in surrender and ecstasy. Thus his music helped him and inspired him on his spiritual journey. A longing for contact with holy men had already developed when he was a boy. His parents brought him to many yogis and sages, Hindu, Muslim, and Parsi, and he loved to sit with them very silently.

When Maula Bakhsh died in 1896, when Inayat was 14, his father took him on a trip to Nepal where there was to be a meeting of musicians. In the mountains of Nepal he met a wonderful old Sufi master, whose glance gave him a feeling of exaltation. He came back, played his vina for him and received a great blessing. He began to meditate more and more, and when, after his return a year later, he also lost his mother, who was very dear to him, he traveled alone all through India, meeting many sages. He began to hear a call during the night as an appeal to him to meditate. And one day, sitting silently with closed eyes, he saw a beautiful face and understood that he had reached a point where he should look for a *murshid*. He went to a great sage in Hyderabad, who felt that he did not deserve the privilage of initiating him. Then a heavenly personality came to visit the sage, and Inayat recognized the face that he had seen in his meditation. Their glances met; there was a deep contact, and Inayat was initiated immediately. From that moment he was completely devoted to his murshid, Mohammed Abu Hashim Madani. He stayed with him for months with an open heart to absorb—mostly in silence—the radiant atmosphere of his murshid. His respect and veneration were unlimited. He experienced what real discipleship could give. But murshid Madani passed away after a relatively short time. This was a very painful loss for Inayat. He left the court of the Nizam of Hyderabad with its grandeur, and followed his desire for solitude and renunciation of worldly life. He went again on a pilgrimage to the holy men of India. He met many of them, had inspiring contacts and many wonderful experiences. His music also deepened more and more. He would quickly rise to the state of samadhi in his music and would create upliftment and ecstasy in his listeners. And yet he began to feel that music had given him all it could, and that a new life's task was coming.

He had lost what was dearest to him in India: his grandfather, Maula Bakhsh, his mother, and his murshid, Abu Hashim Madani. He had renounced his position as a famous singer at the court of Hyderabad, and he saw how music—so sacred to him—began to be used sometimes for superficial entertainment. More and more clearly he began to feel an inner call that had been expressed by his murshid: to go to the West and bring a message of Sufism, harmonizing East and West with his music. And so he left the wonderful world of India behind and traveled to the United States on 13 September 1910, together with his brother Maheboob Khan and his cousin Mohammed Ali Khan; after a short time followed by his younger brother, Musharaff Moulamia Khan.

They found a world completely different from the old India they had left. As Sufism was still quite unknown he started by giving concerts. But this was also difficult. People were not yet used to Indian music. Inayat Khan felt that his music "was put to a hard test." But he met a number of Americans who were interested in it, and some who felt the Sufi message behind it.

One of them was Ora Ray Baker, a young woman who was related to Mary Baker Eddy, the founder of the Christian Science movement. He gave her music lessons. A strong attraction developed between them. She followed him to England and became his wife. They had four children: the eldest, Noorunnisa, followed by Vilayat, Hidayat, and Khairunnisa. Inayat Khan felt that he needed the experience of marriage and children to deepen his understanding of life.

During these first years in the West, Inayat Khan had the opportunity to study the psychology of the people. This was a necessary preparation. The Sufi message had to bring answers to their questions.

After two years in America Inayat Khan and his brothers went to Europe: England, France, and also Russia. Gradually they found some disciples with open hearts who were inspired by Sufism and took up the task of helping to spread the Sufi message.

The First World War was a difficult time, which they spent in London. After the war, when they went back to France, a great outpouring of the Sufi message started in summer schools, first in Katwijk, the Netherlands, then near Paris, and in lectures in many places all over Europe, and during a second trip to the United States. His teachings came as a flow of divine inspiration. More and more disciples were attracted, their questions were answered, and their lives changed. Sufi centers were created in many places and an international organization was established. The Sufi message needed a body, as the human soul needs a body to live on this earthly plane. Therefore the Sufi Movement was established and incorporated in Geneva, Switzerland; and different activities of the Sufi Movement were created.

This fast-growing work took up more and more of Inayat Khan's time. He slept little and could only give very short interviews to the many who were attracted to his radiant personality.

So he had to make a final sacrifice: he renounced his music. He described this himself in the following moving words:

> To serve God one must sacrifice the dearest thing, and I sacrificed my music, the dearest thing to me.
>
> Now, if I do anything, it is to tune souls instead of instruments, to harmonize people instead of notes. If there is anything in my philosophy, it is the law of harmony: that one must put oneself in harmony with oneself and with others.
>
> I played the vina until my heart turned into the same instrument. Then I offered this instrument to the divine Musician, the only musician existing. Since then I have become His flute, and when He chooses He plays His music.[2]

Memories from these years indeed reflect something of this divine music, the heavenly atmosphere of the meditative meetings in the summer school. As one of his early mureeds described it, "Sitting silently in that atmosphere of the divine, before we one by one were allowed for a few minutes in Murshid's presence. The glance which Murshid cast at us, the liberating feeling of purification, surpassing everything, it is all difficult to describe."

It was an indescribable richness. But it could not last. In September 1926 Pir-o-Murshid Hazrat Inayat Khan returned to India hoping to find some rest after his exhausting work for the Sufi message. He was discovered, however, and invited to give lectures in Indian universities. He caught a serious illness and passed away unexpectedly on 5 February 1927. He was only 44 years old, but the Sufi Message he left behind was complete, covering all aspects of life and of the manifestation.

What is the character of this Sufi message? The core of it, of course, is mysticism. As a realized mystic, looking at Western culture, what Hazrat Inayat Khan was destined to do was to open a path to inner realization that so many in the West could not find anymore. He was inspired to invoke the mysteries and

the beauty of that path in many ways. He described the successive steps the seeker for truth has to go through. And he created
the inner school of the Sufi Movement, the Sufi Order, to give
personal guidance to sincere seekers. To initiates in this inner
school he offered the possibility to develop the discipleship that
has always been so important on the mystical path, and a range
of spiritual practices that can help to open the heart and the
inner senses but are also suitable for Westerners who remain
active in worldly life. For an essential aspect of his teaching was
balance. He did not advocate withdrawing from the world in
order to focus only on the inner life: on prayer, contemplation,
and meditation. He shows us a *human* way, living in the world,
meeting our obligations to our fellow human beings with sympathy and understanding—and at the same time learning to
turn within and to come in touch with the peace and inspiration
of the divine light. Then we discover the fullness of life. We can
reach a balance between the inner life, where we open our hearts
in passive surrender to the divine spirit, and the outer life,
where we have to work actively to achieve our ideals and meet
our obligations. Then our actions can be guided by the inspiration and wisdom we receive in our inner attunement, which will
more and more shine through our outer work.

This mystical vision illuminates the whole of life: religion,
philosophy, and psychology. The mystical path is also the essence of *religion*. For the purpose of the inner life—as Hazrat
Inayat Khan puts it—is to make God a reality. Not a theory, a
dogma, or an abstraction, but the deepest experience we can
have. This vision then leads to understanding the fundamental
unity of all the great religions. For these religions have all been
brought to humanity by successive messengers in different ages
to awaken the feeling and realization of the divine. Inayat Khan
shows that the God ideal is a great help for this, but that we
have to realize that it can only be a help, a stepping-stone: that
the divine Reality is beyond our limited intelligence and can

only be experienced in the depths of our being, our soul, which itself is a spark of the divine light. Then we can see all religions as converging ways to the same goal. To express this idea, Hazrat Inayat Khan created the Universal Worship, in which all religions are brought together in a ritual that shows how they are all kindled from the same divine light.

The *philosophical aspect* of the Sufi message is also important. The tremendous development of science and technology in the present time has made it difficult for many people to find their way to religion and to the inner life. For traditional religious dogmas and representations are at odds with modern scientific insight. But Hazrat Inayat Khan's mystical philosophy is completely in line with the deepening understanding of modern science.

The human way that the Sufi message shows means that through the experience and difficulties of the outer life we can make progress toward the inner goal. This is the *psychological aspect* of Inayat Khan's teachings. Here he gives a remarkable insight into the working of our mind. He shows the importance of the impressions which we receive constantly through the outer world, which will be registered in our memory and become living, influencing our feelings, thoughts, words, and actions. And he explains how we can learn to control our mind, allowing only the positive and desirable impressions to live and work within us. By controlling our mind we can then control our life. But as important as the impressions are in our life, they are still only reflections on the mirror of our soul, our inner consciousness. The soul itself remains always pure. Its nature is divine; and it is that divine nature that we have to discover in life.

In their *moral aspect* Hazrat Inayat Khan's teachings also describe a way of gradual progress, of evolution. He speaks about "moral culture" and "the cultivation of the heart." We must learn to understand other people and their points of view, to develop consideration and sympathy for them. That widens our consciousness and helps to overcome the identification with our limited being, the great illusion which blocks our way to the knowledge of God.

All this can only be hinted at in the briefest way in introducing this book in which some of Hazrat Inayat Khan's important teachings on the subject of mysticism are presented. The first part, "The Inner Life," is a powerful evocation of the character of this inner life, which is described as a journey, and of the preparations and conditions which have to be fulfilled if we are to pursue this journey successfully. It shows the beauty of the balance between the inner and outer life and describes how our outlook in life will begin to change when we follow this path.

"Sufi Mysticism" discusses many aspects of the mystical path in its depths and richness. It describes the stages that bring one to realization, the final step, where, as Inayat Khan said, "The mystic is no longer the knower of truth, but truth itself."

The last part, "The Path of Initiation and Discipleship," clarifies these concepts which are so essential on the mystical path. They are often difficult to understand for Western people. But it is natural on the spiritual path that successive initiations reveal to us further mysteries and bring us closer to the divine spirit within and without. And discipleship means opening one's heart in trust to a spiritual guide who has come a little further on the path and can inspire us and help us to overcome the many limitations and attachments in our mind which block progress.

These three essays have earlier been published in volume one and volume ten of *The Sufi Message of Hazrat Inayat Khan,* published for the Sufi Movement.[3] One further hitherto unpublished lecture on the path of the mystic, and some aphorisms, have been added to these essays. The texts of "The Inner Life" and of "Sufi Mysticism" have undergone some minor revisions to bring them closer to the original text of the lectures as Hazrat Inayat Khan gave them.

The words of a mystic have a special power, a fragrance and rhythm which help to disclose the mystery hidden behind them. Their authenticity must therefore be preserved as much as possible. It is for this reason that we have not changed the text in connection with the gender problem, although we see the importance of the balance between the male and female aspect. Inayat Khan, as was customary in his time, often used the masculine in words like *man, brotherhood,* and he referred to God as *he.* But in fact, he was very progressive in this respect, giving women a completely equal position in all activities of his Sufi Movement. During his lifetime his highest initiates were women, who have been among his most important leaders and workers. And in his prayer for peace he addressed himself to the Lord, our Father and Mother.

God is one, manifesting himself in duality.

H.J.W.

NOTES

1. The material for this biographical sketch has been taken from *The Biography of Pir-o-Murshid Hazrat Inayat Khan* (London and The Hague: East West Publication Company).

2. Hazrat Inayat Khan, *The Mysticism of Sound and Music* (Boston: Shambhala Publications, 1996).

3. *The Sufi Message* volumes are now distributed by East West Publications, London and The Hague; and Omega Publications, New Lebanon, New York.

THE INNER LIFE

The Preparation for the Journey

T HE INNER LIFE is a journey, and before starting to take it there is a certain preparation necessary. If one is not prepared, there is always the risk of having to return before one has arrived at one's destination. When a person goes on a journey and when he has to accomplish something, he must know what is necessary on the path, and what he must take with him in order that his journey may become easy and that he may accomplish what he has started to accomplish. The journey one takes in the inner life is as long as the distance between life and death, it being the longest journey one ever takes throughout life. One must have everything prepared, so that after reaching a certain distance one may not have to turn back.

The first thing that is necessary is to see that there is no debt to be paid. Every soul has a certain debt to pay in life; it may be to his mother or father, his brother or sister, to his husband or wife or friend, or to his children, his race or to humanity. If he has not paid what is due, then there are cords with which he is inwardly tied, and they pull him back. Life in the world is fair trade; if one could only understand it, if one knew how many souls there are in this world with whom one is connected or related in some way, or whom one meets freshly every day—to everyone there is something due, and if one has not paid one's obligations, the result is that afterwards one has to pay with interest.

There is the inner justice which is working beyond the worldly justice, and when man does not observe that inner law of justice, it is because at that time he is intoxicated, his eyes are closed, and he really does not know the law of life. But that intoxication will not last; there will come a day when the eyes of every soul will be opened, and it is a pity if the eyes open when it is too late. It is better that the eyes are opened while the purse is full, for it will be very difficult if the eyes open at the time when the purse is empty. To some, consideration is due, to some respect, to some service, to some tolerance, to some forgiveness, to some help. In some way or other, in every relationship, in every connection there is something to pay, and one must know before starting the journey that one has paid it, and be sure that one has paid it in full, so there is nothing more to be paid. Besides this it is necessary that man realizes before starting his journey that he has fulfilled his duties, his duty to those around him and his duty to God. But the one who considers his duty to those around him sacredly does his duty to God.

Man must also consider before starting on his journey whether he has learned all he desired to learn from this world. If there is anything he has not learned, he must finish it before starting the journey, for if he thinks, "I will start the journey, although I had the desire to learn something before starting," in that case he will not be able to reach his goal. That desire to learn something will draw him back. Every desire, every ambition, every aspiration that he has in life must be gratified. Not only this, man must have no remorse of any kind when starting on this journey and no repentance afterwards. If there is any repentance or remorse it must be finished before starting. There must be no grudge against anybody, and no complaining of anyone having done him harm, for all these things which belong to this world, if man took them along, would become a burden on the spiritual path. The journey is difficult enough, and it becomes more difficult if there is a burden to be carried. If a person is lifting a burden of displeasure, dissatisfaction, discomfort, it is difficult to bear it on that path. It is a path to freedom, and to start on this path to freedom man must free himself; no attachment should pull him back, no pleasure should lure him back.

Besides this preparation one needs a vehicle, a vehicle in which he journeys. That vehicle has two wheels, and they are balanced in all things. A man who is one-sided, however great his power of clairvoyance or claraudience, whatever be his knowledge, is yet limited, he cannot go very far, for it requires two wheels for the vehicle to run. There must be a balance, the balance of the head and the heart, the balance of power and wisdom, the balance of activity and repose. It is the balance which enables man to stand the strain of this journey and permits him to go forward, making his path easy. Never imagine for one moment that those who show lack of balance can ever proceed further on the spiritual journey, however greatly in appearance they may seem to be spiritually inclined. It is only the balanced ones who are capable of experiencing the external life as fully as the inner life, to enjoy thought as much as feeling, to rest as well as to act. The center of life is rhythm, and rhythm causes balance.

On this journey certain coins are necessary also, to spend on the way. And what are these coins? They are thoughtful expressions in word and in action. On this journey man must take provision to eat and drink, and that provision is life and light. On this journey man has to take something in which to clothe himself against wind and storm, heat and cold, and that garment is the vow of secrecy, the tendency to silence. On this journey man has to bid farewell to others when starting, and that farewell is loving detachment; before starting on this journey he has to leave something behind with his friends, and that is happy memories of the past.

We are all on the journey; life itself is a journey. No one is settled here, we are all passing onward, and therefore it is not true to say that if we are taking a spiritual journey we have to break our settled life; there is no one living a settled life here; all

are unsettled, all are on their way. Only, by taking the spiritual
journey you are taking another way, one which is easier, better
and more pleasant. Those who do not take this way also will
come in the end; the difference is in the way. One way is easier,
smoother, better; the other is full of difficulties, and as life has
no end of difficulties from the time you have opened your eyes
on this earth, you may just as well choose the smoother way to
arrive at the destination at which all souls will some time arrive.

By "inner life" is meant a life directed towards perfection,
which may be called the perfection of love, harmony, and
beauty; in the words of the orthodox, directed toward God.

The inner life is not necessarily in an opposite direction to
the worldly life, but the inner life is a fuller life. The worldly life
means the limitedness of life; the inner life means a complete
life. The ascetics who have taken a direction quite opposite to
the worldly life have done so in order to have the facility to
search into the depths of life, but going in one direction alone
does not make a complete life. Therefore the inner life means
the fullness of life.

In brief one may say that the inner life consists of two things:
action with knowledge, and repose with passivity of mind. By
accomplishing these two contrary motions, and by keeping balanced in these two directions, one comes to the fullness of life.
A person who lives the inner life is as innocent as a child; even
more innocent than a child, but at the same time more wise
than many clever people put together. This shows as a development in two contrary directions. The innocence of Jesus has
been known through the ages. In his every movement, in his
every action, he showed himself to be as a child. All the great
saints and sages, the great ones who have liberated humanity,
have been as innocent as children and at the same time wiser,
much more so than the worldly-wise. And what makes it so?
What gives them this balance? It is repose with passiveness.
When they stand before God they stand with their heart as an

empty cup; when they stand before God to learn, they unlearn all things that the world has taught them; when they stand before God, their ego, their self, their life, is no more before them. They do not think of themselves in that moment with any desire to be fulfilled, with any motive to be accomplished, with any expression of their own, but as empty cups that God may fill their being, that they may lose the false self.

Therefore the same thing helps them in their everyday life to show a glimpse of the quiet moment of repose they had with God. They show in their everyday life innocence, and yet not ignorance; they know things and they do not know. They know if somebody is telling a lie, but do they accuse that person, do they say, "You are telling a lie"? They are above it. They know all the plays of the world, and they look at them all passively; they rise above things of this world which make no impression on them. They take people quite simply. Some may think that they are ignorant in their world-lives, that they take no notice of things that are of no importance. Activity with wisdom makes them more wise, because it is not everybody in this world who directs his every action with wisdom. There are many who never consult wisdom in their action; there are others who seek refuge under wisdom after their action, and very often it is then too late. But the ones who live the inner life all direct their activity with wisdom; every movement, every action, every thought, every word is first thought out, is first weighed and measured and analysed before it is expressed. Therefore in the world everything they do is with wisdom, but before God they stand with innocence, there they do not take worldly wisdom.

Man often makes mistakes, either by taking one way or the other, and therefore he lacks balance and he does not come to touch perfection. For instance, when he takes the way of activity in the path of God, he also wishes to use his wisdom there; in the path of God also he wishes to be active where he does not need action. It is just like swimming against the tide; where you must be innocent, if you use your wisdom there, it is the greatest error. Then there are others who are accustomed to take as a principle the passivity with which they stand before God in their innocence, and they wish to use the same principle in all directions of life, which would not be right.

II

The Object of the Journey

THE FIRST AND PRINCIPAL THING in the inner life is to establish a relationship with God, making God the object which we relate to, such as the Creator, Sustainer, Forgiver, Judge, Friend, Father, Mother and Beloved. In every relation we must place God before us, and become conscious of that relation so that it will no more remain an imagination, for the first thing a believer does is to imagine. He imagines that God is the Creator and tries to believe that God is the Sustainer; he makes an effort to think that God is a Friend, and an attempt to feel that he loves God. But if this imagination is to become a reality, then exactly as one feels for one's earthly beloved sympathy, love and attachment, so one must feel the same for God. However pious, good or righteous a person may be, yet without this his piety or his goodness are not a reality to him.

The work of the inner life is to make God a reality, so that He is no more an imagination; that this relation that man has with God may seem to him more real than any other relation in this world. And when this happens then all relationships, however near and dear, become less binding. But at the same time a person does not thus become cold, he becomes more loving. It is the godless man who is cold, impressed by the selfishness and lovelessness of this world, because he partakes of those conditions in which he lives. But the one who is in love with God, the one who has established his relationship with God, his love becomes living, he is no more cold; he fulfils his duties to those related to him in this world much more than does the godless man.

Now, as to the way in which man establishes this relationship, which is the most desirable to establish with God, what should he imagine? God as Father, as Creator, as Judge, as Forgiver, as Friend, or as Beloved? The answer is, that in every capacity of life we must give God the place that is demanded by the moment. When, crushed by the injustice, the coldness of the world, man looks at God, the perfection of justice, he no more remains agitated, his heart is no more disturbed, he consoles himself with the justice of God. He places the just God before him, and by this he learns justice. The sense of justice awakens in his heart, and he sees things in quite a different light.

When man finds himself in this world motherless or fatherless, then he thinks that there is the mother and father in God; and even if he were in the presence of his mother and father, these are only related on earth. The motherhood and fatherhood of God is the only real relationship. The mother and father of the earth reflect only a spark of that motherly and fatherly love which God has in fullness and perfection. Then man finds that God can forgive, as the parents can forgive the child if he was in error. Then man feels the goodness, kindness, protection, support, sympathy, coming from every side; he learns to feel that it comes from God, the Father-Mother through all.

When man pictures God as Forgiver, he finds that there is not only in this world a strict justice, but there is love developed also, there is mercy and compassion, there is that sense of forgiveness, that God is not the servant of law as is the judge in this world, He is Master of law; He judges when He judges, when He forgives He forgives; He has both powers, He has the power to judge and He has the power to forgive. He is Judge because He does not close His eyes to all man does; He knows, He weighs and measures and He returns what is due to man. He is Forgiver because beyond and above His power of justice there is His great power of love and compassion which is His very being, which is His own nature, and therefore it is more, and in greater proportion and working with a greater activity than His power of justice. We, the human beings in this world, if there is a spark of goodness or kindness in our hearts, avoid judging people. We prefer forgiving to judging. Forgiving gives us naturally a greater happiness than taking revenge, unless a man is on quite a different path.

The man who realizes God as a friend is never lonely in the world, neither in this world nor in the hereafter. There is always a friend, a friend in the crowd, a friend in the solitude, or while he is asleep, unconscious of this outer world, and when he is awake and conscious of it; in both cases the friend is there in his thought, in his imagination, in his heart, in his soul.

The man who makes God his Beloved, what more does he want? His heart becomes awakened to all the beauty there is within and without. To him all things appeal, everything unfolds itself, and it is beauty to his eyes, because God is all-pervading, in all names and all forms; therefore his Beloved is never absent. How happy therefore is the one whose Beloved is never absent, because the whole tragedy of life is the absence of the Beloved, and to one whose Beloved is always there, when he has closed his eyes the Beloved is within, when he has opened his eyes the Beloved is without. His every sense perceives the Beloved; his eyes see Him, his ears hear His voice. When a person arrives at this realization, then he, so to speak, lives in the presence of God; then to him the different forms and beliefs, faiths and communities do not count. To him God is all-in-all; to him God is everywhere. If he goes to the Christian church or to the synagogue, to the Buddhist temple, to the Hindu shrine, or to the mosque of the Muslim, there is God. In the wilderness, in the forest, in the crowd, everywhere he sees God.

This shows that the inner life does not consist in closing the eyes and looking inward. The inner life is to look outwardly *and* inwardly and to find one's beloved everywhere. But God cannot be made a Beloved unless the love element is awakened sufficiently. The one who hates his enemy and loves his friend cannot call God his Beloved, for he does not know God. When love comes to its fullness, then one looks at the friend with affection, on the enemy with forgiveness, on the stranger with sympathy. There is love in all its aspects expressed when love rises to its fullness, and it is the fullness of love which is worth offering to God. It is then that man recognizes in God his Beloved, his Ideal, and by that, although he rises above the narrow affection of this world, in reality he is the one who knows how to love even his friend. It is the lover of God who knows love when he rises to that stage of the fullness of love.

The whole imagery of the Sufi literature in the Persian language, written by great poets, such as Rumi, Hafiz, and Jami, is the relationship between man as the lover and God as Beloved. When one reads understanding that, and develops in that affection, then one sees what pictures the mystics have made and to what note their heart has been tuned. It is not easy to develop in the heart the love of God, because when one does not see or realize the object of love, one cannot love. God must become tangible in order that one may love Him, but once a person has attained to love God, he has really entered the journey of the spiritual path.

III

Fulfilment of the Obligations of Human Life

THE POSITION OF THE PERSON living the inner life becomes like that of a grown-up person living among many children. At the same time, outwardly there seems no such difference as is apparent in the ages of the children and the grown person, the difference lying in the size of his outlook which is not always apparent. One who lives the inner life becomes much older than those around him, and yet outwardly he is the same as every other person. Therefore the man who has arrived at the fullness of the inner life adopts quite a different policy from the one who is just beginning to tread that path, and also a different one from that of the man who knows intellectually something about the inner life, but who does not really live it. The action again is different in the world, for the latter will criticize others who do not know what he thinks he knows, and will look upon them with pride and conceit, or with contempt, thinking that they have not risen to the mystery, to the height to which he has risen, and which he understands. He wishes to disconnect himself from people, saying that they are backward in their evolution, and that he cannot go with them. He says, "I am more advanced; I cannot join them in anything; they are different, I am different." He laughs at the petty ideas of those who surround him, and looks upon them as human beings with whom he must not associate, with whom he must not join in all the things they do because he is much more advanced than they are.

But for the one who comes to the fullness of the inner life it is a great joy to mingle with his fellow-man, just as it is for parents to play with their little children; the best moments of their lives are when they feel as a child with their children and when they can join in their play. Parents who are kind and loving, if a child brings them a doll's cup, will pretend that they are drinking tea and that they are enjoying it; they do not let the child think that they are superior, or that this is something in which they must not join. They play with the child, and they are happy with it, because the happiness of the children is theirs also.

That is the action of the man who lives the inner life, and it is for this reason that he agrees and harmonizes with people of all grades of evolution, whatever be their ideas, their thoughts, their belief, or their faith, in whatever form they worship or show their religious enthusiasm. He does not say, "I am much more advanced than you are, and to join you would be going backwards." The one who has gone so far forward can never go backwards, but by joining them he takes them along with him, onward. If he went on alone he would consider that he avoided his duty towards his fellow-man, which he should perform. It is the empty pitcher that makes a noise when you knock upon it, but the pitcher which is full of water does not make any sound, it is silent, speechless.

So the wise live among all the people of this world, and they are not unhappy. The one who loves all is not unhappy. Unhappy is he who looks with contempt at the world, who hates human beings and thinks he is superior to them; the one who loves them thinks only that they are going through the same process that he has gone through. It is from the darkness that he has to come into the light. It is just a difference of moments, and he with great patience passes those moments while his fellow-men are still in darkness, not making them know that they are in darkness, not letting them feel hurt about it, not looking upon them with contempt, only thinking that for every soul there is childhood, there is youth and maturity. So it is natural for every human being to go through this process. I have seen with my own eyes souls who have attained saintliness and who have reached great perfection; and yet such a soul would stand before the idol of stone with a fellow-man and worship, not letting him know that he was in any way more advanced than other men, keeping himself in a humble guise, not making any pretence that he had gone further in his spiritual evolution.

The further such souls go, the more humble they become; the greater the mystery they have realized, the less they speak about it. You would scarcely believe it if I were to tell you that during four years of the presence of my Murshid, hardly more than once or twice did I have a conversation on spiritual matters. Usually the conversation was on worldly things, like everybody else's; nobody would perceive that here was a God-realized man who was always absorbed in God. His conversation was like that of every other person, he spoke on everything belonging to this world, never a spiritual conversation, nor any special show of piety, or spirituality, and yet his atmosphere, the voice of his soul and his presence revealed all that was hidden in his heart.

Those who are God-realized and those who have touched wisdom speak very little of the subject. It is those who do not know who try to discuss it, not because they know, but because they themselves have doubts. When there is knowledge there is satisfaction, there is no tendency towards dispute. When one disputes, it is because there is something not satisfied. There is nothing in this world, wealth or rank, position, power, or learning that can give such conceit as the slightest little amount of spiritual knowledge, and once a person has that conceit, then he cannot take a further step; he is nailed down to that place where he stands, because the very idea of spiritual realization is in selflessness. Man has either to realize himself as something, or as nothing. In this realization of nothingness there is spirituality. If one has any little knowledge of the inner laws of nature and is proud of it, or if one has any sense of thinking, "How good I am, how kind I am, how generous, how well-mannered, how influential, how attractive," the slightest idea of anything of this kind coming into the mind closes the doors which lead into the spiritual world. It is such an easy path to tread and yet so difficult. Pride is so natural to a human being, man may deny a virtue a thousand times in words, but he cannot help admitting it with his feelings, for the ego itself is pride. Pride *is* the ego, man cannot live without it. In order to attain to spiritual knowledge, in order to become conscious of the inner life, one does not need to learn very much, because here he has to know what he already knows. Only, he has to discover it himself. For his understanding of spiritual knowledge he does not need the knowledge of anything except himself. He acquires the knowledge of the self, which is himself—so near and yet so far.

Another thing the lover of God shows is the same tendency as the human lover shows. He does not talk about his love to anybody; he cannot talk about it. Man cannot say how much he loves his beloved, no words can express it, and besides, he does not feel like talking about it to anybody. Even if he could, in the presence of his beloved he would close his lips. How then could the lover of God make a profession, "I love God!" The true lover of God keeps his love silently hidden in his heart, like a seed sown in the ground, and if the seedling grows, it grows in his actions towards his fellow-man. He cannot act except with kindness, he cannot feel anything but forgiveness; every movement he makes, everything he does, speaks of his love, but not his lips.

This shows that in the inner life the greatest principle that one should observe is to be unassuming, quiet, without any show of wisdom, without any manifestation of learning, without any desire to let anyone know how far one has advanced, not even letting oneself know how far one has gone. The task to be accomplished is the entire forgetting of oneself and harmonizing with one's fellow-man; acting in agreement with all, meeting everyone on his own plane, speaking to everyone in his own tongue, answering the laughter of one's friends with a smile, and the pain of another with tears, standing by one's friends in their joy and their sorrow, whatever be one's own grade of evolution. If a man through his life became like an angel, he would accomplish very little. The accomplishment which is most desirable for man is to fulfil the obligations of human life.

IV

The Realization of the Inner Life

THE PRINCIPLE OF THE ONE who experiences the inner life, is to become all things to all men throughout his life. In every situation, in every capacity, he answers the demand of the moment. Often people think that the spiritual person must be a man with sad looks, with a long face, with a serious expression and with a melancholy atmosphere. Really speaking, that picture is the exact contrary of the real spiritual person. In all capacities the one who lives the inner life has to act outwardly as he ought in order to fit the occasion; he must act according to the circumstances, and he must speak to everyone in his own language, standing upon the same level, and yet realizing the inner life.

For the knower of truth, the one who has attained spiritual knowledge and who lives the inner life, there is no occupation in life which is too difficult; as a business man, as a professional man, as a king, a ruler, a poor man, a worldly man, as a priest or monk, in all aspects he is different from what people know and see of him. To the one who lives the inner life the world is a stage, on which he is the actor who has to act a part in which he has sometimes to be angry and sometimes loving, and in which he has to take part both in tragedy and comedy. So also the one who has realized the inner life acts constantly; and like the actor who does not feel the emotions he assumes, the spiritual man has to fill fittingly the place in which life has placed him. There he performs everything thoroughly and rightly, in order to fulfil his outer mission in life. He is a friend to his friend, a relative to his relatives. With all to whom he is outwardly related he keeps the right relationship with thought, with consideration, and yet in his realization he is above all relationships. He is in the crowd and in the solitude at the same time. He may be very much amused and at the same time he is very serious. He may seem very sad and yet there is joy welling up from his heart.

Therefore the one who has realized the inner life is a mystery to everyone; no one can fathom the depth of that person, except that he promises sincerity, he emits love, he commands trust, he spreads goodness, and he gives an impression of God and the truth. For the man who has realized the inner life every act is his meditation; if he is walking in the street it is his meditation; if he is working as a carpenter, as a goldsmith or in any other trade or business, that is his meditation. It does not matter if he is looking at heaven or at the earth, he is looking at the object that he worships. East or west or north or south, upon all sides is his God. In form, in principle, nothing restricts him. He may know things and yet may not speak, for if a man who lives the inner life were to speak of his experiences it would confuse many minds.

There are some individuals in the world who from morning until evening have their eyes and their ears focused on every dark corner, wanting to listen, or to see what they can find out; and they find out nothing. If someone were to tell such people

wonders, he would have a very good occupation, the whole
world would seek him. But such is not the work of the self-
realized man. He sees and yet does not look; if he were to look,
how much he would see! There is so much to be seen by one
whose every glance, wherever it is cast, breaks through every
object and discovers its depth and its secret. And if he were to
look at things and find out their secrets and depths where would
it end, and of what interest is it to him?

The inner life, therefore, is seeing all things and yet not
seeing them, feeling all things and not expressing them, for they
cannot be fully expressed; understanding all things and not explaining; how far can such a man explain, and how much can
another understand? Each according to the capacity he has, no
more. The inner life is not lived by closing the eyes; one need
not close one's eyes from this world in order to live it, one can
just as well open them.

The exact meaning of the inner life is not only to live in the
body, but to live in the heart, to live in the soul. Why then does
not the average man live the inner life when he too has a heart
and a soul? It is because he has a heart and yet is not conscious
of it; he has a soul and knows not what it is. When he lives in
the captivity of the body, limited by that body, he can only feel
a thing by touching it, he sees only by looking through his eyes,
he hears only by hearing with his ears. How much can the ears
hear and the eyes see? All this experience obtained by the outer
senses is limited. When man lives in this limitation he does not
know that another part of his being exists, which is much
higher, more wonderful, more living, and more exalted. Once
he begins to know this then the body becomes his tool, for he
lives in his heart. And then later he passes on and lives in his
soul. He experiences life independently of his body, and that is
called the inner life. Once man has experienced the inner life
the fear of death has expired, for he knows death comes to the
body, not to his inner being. When once he begins to realize life

in his heart and in his soul, then he looks upon his body as a coat. If the coat is old he puts it away and takes a new one, for his being does not depend upon his coat. The fear of death lasts only so long as man has not realized that his real being does not depend upon his body.

Therefore the joy of the one who experiences the inner life is beyond comparison greater than that of the average man living only as a captive in his mortal body. Yet the inner life does not necessitate man's adopting a certain way of living, or living an ascetic or a religious life. Whatever his outer occupation be it does not matter; the man who lives the inner life lives it through all. Man always looks for a spiritual person in a religious person, or perhaps in what he calls a good person, or in someone with a philosophical mind, but that is not necessarily the case. A person may be religious, even philosophical, a person may be religious or good, and yet he may not live the inner life.

There is no distinct outward appearance which can prove a person to be living the inner life, except one thing. When a child grows toward youth, you can see in the expression of that child a light beaming out, a certain new consciousness arising, a new knowledge coming which the child has not known before. That is the sign of youth, yet the child does not say so; he cannot say it, even if he wanted to he cannot explain it. And yet you can see it from every movement that the child makes; from his every expression you can find that he is realizing life now. So it is with the soul; when the soul begins to realize the life above and beyond this life, it begins to show. And although the man who realizes this may refrain from purposely showing it, yet from his expression, his movement, his glance, his voice, from every action he does and from every attitude, the wise can grasp and the others can feel that he is conscious of some mystery.

The inner life is a birth of the soul, as Christ said that unless the soul is born again it cannot enter the kingdom of heaven.

Therefore the realization of the inner life is entering the kingdom of heaven; and when this consciousness comes to the
human being it shows itself as a new birth, and with this new
birth there comes the assurance of everlasting life.

V

Freedom of Action

A s man grows through the inner life, so he feels a freedom of thought, speech, and action which comes as a natural course through his spiritual journey. And the reason why
this freedom comes and whence it comes can be explained by
the fact that there is a spirit of freedom hidden within man,
covered by outward conventionalities. When man grows out of
the outward conventionalities, then the spirit of freedom, which
was closed in so far, becomes manifest.

The laws given to humanity are given by those far from such
laws, the Elder Ones. As for children, there are certain laws,
certain rules necessary, so those who have not yet evolved to
look at life from the higher point of view are fixed under certain
laws which are taught to them as religion; and they are as necessary for mankind as the rules given to the children in the home.
If there were no rules given, the children would become unruly;
but when the children become grown-up then they begin to see
for themselves the reason why rules were given to them and the
benefit that these rules were to them; then they can make such
rules for themselves as suit them best.

The inner life helps a soul to grow up; when the soul evolves
from subjection to mastery, then it makes rules for itself. In the
East, therefore, no one tries to criticize a spiritual person; no

one stands up to judge his action or to accuse him of something which he himself calls wrong. For this reason Jesus Christ has said, "Judge not." But this teaching has been given to point out that "judge not" applies to your equal; for the one who is still more advanced no one can judge. When man has the tendency to judge one more advanced than himself, the consequence is that spiritual advancement deteriorates; because however advanced he may be, those who have not yet advanced pull him down. Therefore humanity instead of going forward goes backward. What happened in the case of Jesus Christ? He was judged. The liberated soul, the soul which was made free by divine nature, was judged at the court of man. Men less advanced considered themselves sufficiently learned to judge Christ, and not only to judge, but to give sentence.

In whatever period of civilization, therefore, when the tendency to judge the one who is advanced has shown itself, there has always come a collapse of the whole civilization. The Sufi Sarmad, a great saint who lived in Gwalior, was asked by the Emperor Aurangzeb to attend at the mosque, for it was against the rules of the time that anyone kept away from the regular prayers, which took place in the mosque of the state. Sarmad being a man of ecstasy, living every moment of his day and night in union with God, being God-conscious himself, perhaps forgot, or refused; a certain time of prayer or a certain place for prayer to him was nothing. Every place to him was a place of prayer, every time was a time of prayer; his every breath was a prayer. As he refused to attend prayers he was beheaded for going against the rules which were made for everyone. The consequence was the downfall of the whole Mogul Empire, which can be dated from that time; the entire Mogul civilization, unique in its time, fell to pieces.

The Hindus have always known this philosophy, for the reason that they had a perfect religion, a religion in which one aspect of God was characterized as human, and their various *devas* are nothing but various characteristics of human nature, each of them adored and worshipped. In this way not only God, but the whole human nature in all its aspects, was adored and worshipped. It is that which makes the Hindu religion perfect. When people say, "This place is sacred, and the other place is not sacred; that particular thing is holy, and all other things not holy," in this way they divide life into many pieces, the life which is one, the life which cannot be divided.

Therefore those who rise above the ordinary conventionalities of life by their inner development come to another consciousness. For them worldly laws are the laws for the children. Those who begin to see this difference between the laws they set before themselves and the laws that are observed by mankind, at first sometimes condemn and then disregard the common laws. They criticize them and ask, "What is it all for?" But those who come to the fuller realization of the inner laws show respect even for the laws of the children; knowing that they *are* the laws for the children and not for the grown-ups, yet they respect them, for they know that it cannot be otherwise. The laws which they know can only manifest to the one whose soul rises to that realization, but before that soul rises it must have some law by which to live in harmony. Therefore advanced souls regard such laws with respect, and observe them when they are in the community. They do not condemn them, they will not criticize them. They realize that harmony is the principal thing in life and that we cannot be happy through life if we cannot harmonize with all those around us. Whatever be our grade of evolution, whatever be our outlook on life, and whatever be our freedom, we must have regard for the laws of the majority.

Now the question is: do those who are spiritually advanced have any special conception of morals? Indeed they have, and their morals are great morals, much greater than the average human being can conceive of. It is not that by becoming free spiritually from the laws of the generality, they become free from their own laws. They have their own laws to bind them, and these are much higher and much greater laws. No doubt their way of looking at things may be criticized and may not be generally understood. Yet their law is more akin to nature; their laws are in harmony with the spirit; their laws have their effect as phenomena; and by regarding two morals which are contrary to each other, the morals of the generality and their own morals, they arrive at a plane and a condition where their hands and feet are nailed. That is the symbolic meaning of the nailing of Christ to the cross.

VI

The Law of the Inner Life

THOSE WHO LIVE THE INNER LIFE begin to see a law which is hidden to the average man. There is the law of nature which is known as science, and that of life which is called moral law; but beyond science and morals there is another law. It may be called occult law, or in other words inner law; a law which can be understood by an open heart and an awakened soul.

This law manifests to the view of the seer in many and varied forms; sometimes it appears in quite a contrary form to the effect that it has later on in its manifestation. The eye of the seer becomes a sword which cuts open, so to speak, all things, including the hearts of men, and sees clearly through all they contain; but it is a cutting open which is at the same time healing.

In the Qur'an it is said that God has taught man by the skill of His pen. And what does that mean? It means that to the man who lives the inner life, everything that he sees becomes a written character and this whole visible world a book. He reads it as plainly as a letter written by his friend. And besides this he hears a voice within—which becomes to him a language. It is an inner language; its words are not the same as the words of the external language. It is a divine language. It is a language without words, which can only be called a voice, and yet it serves as a language. It is like music, which is as clear as a language to the musician. Another person enjoys music, but only the musician knows exactly what it says, what every note is, how it is expressed and what it reveals. Every phrase of music to him has a meaning; every piece of music to him is a picture. But this I say only about a real musician.

People profess to have clairvoyance and clairaudience, and very often delude others by giving false prophecies; but the one who lives the inner life does not need to prophesy, he does not need to tell others what he sees and what he hears. It is not only that he is not inclined to do so, but also he sees no necessity for it; besides, he cannot fully express himself. How difficult it is to translate fully the poetry of one language into the poetry of another! Yet it is only interpreting the ideas of one part of the earth to the people of another part of the same earth. How much more difficult then it must be to translate or to interpret the ideas of the divine world to the human world. In what words can they be given, what phrases can be used for them, and after being given even in words and phrases, who would understand them? It is the language of a different world.

Therefore, when the prophets and seers of all ages have given to humanity a certain message and law, it was only the giving of a drop from the ocean which they received into their hearts. And this also is a great difficulty, for even this drop is not intelligible. Does every Christian understand the Bible? Does every Muslim know the Qur'an, or every Hindu the Vedanta? No, they may know the words of the verses but not always the real meaning. Among the Muslims there are some who know the whole Qur'an by heart, but that does not suffice for the purpose. The whole of nature is a secret book, yet it is an open book to the seer. How can man translate it, how can man interpret it? It is like trying to bring the sea onto the land; one can bring it, but how much?

The understanding of this law gives quite a different outlook on life to the seer, which makes him more inclined to appreciate all that is good and beautiful, to admire all that is worth admiring, to enjoy all that is worth enjoying, to experience all that is worth experiencing. It awakens the sympathy of the seer to love, to tolerate, to forgive, to endure and to sympathize; it gives the inclination to support, to protect, and to serve those in need. But can he say what he really feels, how he really feels? No, he cannot say it even to himself.

Therefore, the one who lives the inner life is all things; he is as a physician who knows things that a physician cannot know, as an astrologer who knows much more than the astrologer, an artist who knows that which an artist could not know, a musician who knows what a musician does not know, a poet who knows what the poet cannot perceive; for he becomes the artist of the entire world, the singer of the divine song, he becomes an astrologer of the entire cosmos, which is hidden to the sight of men. He does not need outer things as the signs of knowing the eternal life. His very life itself is the evidence of the everlasting life. To him death is a shadow, it is a change, it is turning the face from one side to the other. To him all things have their meaning, every movement in this world—the movement of the water, of the air, of the lightning and the thunder and the wind, every movement has a message for him—it brings to him some sign. To another person it is only the thunder, it is only a storm, but to him every movement has its meaning. And when he rises in his development, not only has every movement its meaning, but on every movement there is his command. It is that part of his life which becomes mastership.

Besides this, in all affairs of this world, of individuals and multitudes, which confuse people, which bring them despair and cause them depression, which give joy and pleasure, which amuse them—he sees through all. He knows why it comes, whence it comes, what is behind it, what is the cause of it, and behind the seeming cause what is the hidden cause. If he wished to trace the cause behind the cause he could trace back to the primal cause, for the inner life is lived by living with the primal cause, by being in unity with the primal cause. Therefore the one who lives the inner life, in other words, who lives the life of God, God is in him and he is in God.

VII

The Object of the Inner Life

I S IT POWER WHICH is the object of the spiritual person, or is it inspiration after which he seeks? It is in fact neither of these things which he pursues, but all such things as power and inspiration follow him as he proceeds on his path towards the spiritual goal. The goal of the spiritual person is self-realization, and his journey is towards the depth of his own being, his God, his ideal.

Does such a person sacrifice all interests in life, or does he consider the different objects that people have in their lives as something leading astray? Not at all; no doubt his object is the highest that any soul can have, but all other objects which he sees before himself in life do not necessarily hinder him on his path; they become as a staircase on his way, making his path easy to tread. Therefore the person living the inner life never condemns and does not criticize the objects of another, however small or ridiculous they may appear, for he knows that every object in the life of a person is but a stepping-stone which leads him forward if he only wishes to go forward.

There is a time in the life of a soul when it has the desire to play with dolls; there is a seeking after toys. From the spiritual point of view there is no harm in that, and man sees in time the way that leads to the goal; these are only passing interests leading to others, and in this way man goes forward.

Therefore according to the view of the seer man places before him at different times such objects as riches, pleasure, or a material heaven; the spiritual person starts his journey from the point where these end. The process of evolution is not a straight way, it is more like a wheel which is ever turning. So the experience of the person who treads the spiritual path begins to show a downward tendency and from that again upwards. For instance, in the spiritual path a person goes backwards, he experiences youth again, for spirituality gives health to the mind and to the body, it being the real life. He experiences vigour, strength, aspiration, enthusiasm, energy, and a living spirit that makes him feel youthful whatever be his age. Then he becomes as a little child, eager to play, ready to laugh, happy among children, he shows in his personality childlike traits, especially that look one sees in children, where there is no worry, anxiety, or bitter feeling against anyone; where there is a desire to be friendly with all, where there is no pride or conceit, but readiness to associate with anybody, whatever be his class or caste, nation or race. So the spiritual person becomes like a child; the tendency to tears, the readiness for laughter, all these are found in the spiritual person.

As the spiritual person goes further he shows in his nature infancy. This can be perceived in his innocence; his heart may be lighted with wisdom, yet he is innocent; he is easily deceived, even knowingly, besides being happy under all conditions, like an infant. As the infant has no regard for honour or for insult, neither has the spiritual person. When he arrives at this stage, he answers insult with a smile. Honours given to him are like honours given to a little baby who does not know to whom they are offered. Only the person who has given the honours knows that they have been given to somebody there. The spiritual one is not conscious of it, nor happy with it, nor proud of it. It is nothing to him. The one who has honoured him has honoured himself, since to the baby it is nothing if somebody should speak in favour of him or against him; the baby does not mind, he is ready to smile at both; so is the spiritual soul.

As the spiritual soul proceeds further he begins to show the real traits of humanity, for here humanity really begins. One can see in such a soul the signs which are the pure characteristics of the human being, devoid of the animal traits. For instance, there is a tendency in him to appreciate every little good deed done by anyone, to admire good wherever he sees it in any person, a tendency to sympathize, whatever be the condition of the person, saint or sinner, a tendency to take interest in the affairs of his friends when called upon to do so, a tendency to sacrifice, not considering what he sacrifices, as long as he is moved to do that action. Respect, gratitude, sincerity, faithfulness, patience, endurance, all these qualities begin to show in the character of that man. It is in this stage that truly he can judge, for at this stage the sense of justice awakens.

But as he grows, he still continues to grow backwards. He now shows the signs of the animal kingdom. For instance, such a quality as that of the elephant, which with all its strength and power of giant bulk is ready to take the load put upon it; the horse, which is ready to serve the rider; and the cow, which lives in the world harmoniously, comes home without being driven, gives milk which is the right of her calf. These qualities come to the spiritual person. The same thing is taught by Christ.

When he goes on further still, there develops in him the quality of the vegetable kingdom, of the plants which bring forth fruit and flowers, patiently waiting for the rain from above, never asking any return from those who come to gather flowers and fruit, giving and never expecting a return, desiring only to bring forth beauty according to the capability which is hidden in them, and letting it be taken by the worthy or unworthy, whoever it be, without any expectation of appreciation or thanks.

And when the spiritual person advances still further, he arrives at the stage of the mineral kingdom. He becomes as a rock, a rock for others to lean on, to depend upon, a rock that stands unmoved amidst the constantly moving waves of the sea of life; a rock to endure all things of this world whose influence has a jarring effect upon sensitive human beings; a rock of constancy in friendship, of steadiness in love, of loyalty to every ideal for which he has taken his stand. One can depend upon him through life and death, here and hereafter. In this world where nothing is dependable, which is full of changes every moment, such a soul has arrived at the stage where he shows through all these changes that rock-like quality, proving thereby his advancement to the mineral kingdom.

His further advancement is into the *jinn* quality, which represents the all-knowing, all-understanding. There is nothing he cannot understand; however difficult the situation, however subtle the problem, whatever be the condition of those around him, he understands it all. A man may come to him hardened with faults that he has committed all his life—before this understanding he melts, for whether it be a friend or an enemy, this spiritual person understands both. Not only has he the knowledge of human nature, but of objects as well, of conditions of life in general in all its aspects.

And when he advances still further, his nature develops into that of an angel. The nature of the angel is to be worshipful. He therefore worships God in all creatures; he does not feel to be any greater or better or any more spiritual himself than anybody else. In this realization he is the worshipper of all the names and forms there are, for he considers them all the names and forms of God. There is no one, however degenerate or looked down upon by the world, who is any less in his eyes. In his eyes there is no one but the divine Being, and in this way every moment of his life is devoted to worship. For him it is no longer necessary that he must worship God at a certain time or in a certain house, or in a certain manner. There is not one moment that he is not in worship, every moment of his life he is in worship, he is before God, and being before God at every moment of his life he becomes so purified that his heart becomes a crystal where everything is clear. Everything is reflected there, no one can hide his thoughts from him, nothing is hidden from him, all is known as clearly as it is known to the other person. And more so, for every person knows his own condition and yet not the reason; but the spiritual being at this stage knows the condition of the person and the reason behind it. Therefore he knows more about every person than that person knows himself.

It is in this stage that his progress culminates and comes to its fullness, and concerning this Christ has spoken in the words, "Be ye perfect, as your Father in heaven is perfect." When that stage arrives, it is beyond all expression. It is a sense, it is a realization, it is a feeling, which words can never explain. There is only one thing that can be said: when a person has touched that stage which is called perfection, his thought, speech, action, his atmosphere, everything becomes productive of God; he spreads God everywhere. Even if he did not speak, still he would spread God; if he did not do anything, still he would bring God. And thus those God-realized ones bring to the world the living God. At present there exists in the world only a belief in God; God exists in imagination, in the ideal. It is such a soul which has touched divine Perfection that brings to the earth a living God, who without him would remain only in the heavens.

The Attainment of the Inner Life

I N THE ATTAINMENT OF THE INNER LIFE there are five things necessary. The first thing that is necessary is the mastery of the mind, and this is done by unlearning all one has learned. The inner knowledge is not gained by adding to the knowledge one has already achieved in life, for it requires a rock foundation. One cannot build a house of rocks on a foundation of sand. Therefore in order to make the foundation of rocks, one has to dig into the sand and build the foundation on the rocks below. Very often therefore it becomes difficult for an intellectual person, who through life has learned things and understood them by the power of intellect, to attain to the inner life, for these two paths are different. The one goes to the north and the other goes to the south. When a person says, "I have now walked so many miles to the south, shall I therefore reach sooner something that exists in the north?" he must know that he will not reach it sooner, but later, because as many hours as he has walked to the south he must walk back in order to reach the north.

Therefore it must be understood that all man learns and experiences in this life in the world, all that he calls learning or knowledge, is only used in the world where he is learning, and bears the same relation to himself as the eggshell does to the chick; but when he takes the path to the inner life, that learning and knowledge is of no use to him. The more he is capable of forgetting that knowledge, of unlearning it, the more capable is he of attaining the object for which he treads the spiritual path. Therefore it has been a great struggle for those learned and experienced in the outer life, to think that after their great advancement in worldly knowledge they have to go back again. Often they cannot understand; many among them think it is strange and are therefore disappointed. It is like learning the language of a certain country, when wanting to go into another country where that language is not understood, nor the language of the latter country understood by oneself. Just as there is the north pole and the south pole, so there is the outward and the inward life. The difference is still vaster, because the gap between the inner life and the outer life is vaster than the distance between the north pole and south pole. The one who advances to the south is not getting nearer to the north pole, but on the contrary he is going further from it; in order to reach it he must turn right round. However, it is not difficult for the soul who is an earnest traveller on the path. It is only using the enthusiasm in the opposite direction; to turn the enthusiasm one has for learning something of the world into forgetting and unlearning it, in order to learn something of the inner life.

Now the question is how does one unlearn? Learning is forming a knot in the mind. Whatever one learns from experience or from a person, one makes a knot of it in the mind, and there are as many knots found as there are things one has learned. Unlearning is unravelling the knot, and it is as hard to unlearn as it is to untie a knot. How much effort it requires, how much patience it requires to unravel when one has made a knot and pulled it tight from both sides! So it requires patience and effort to unravel the knots in the mind. And what helps the process? The light of reason working with full power unravels the mental knots. A knot is a limited reason. When one unravels it its limitation is taken away, it is open. When the mind becomes smooth by unlearning, and by digging out all impressions of good and bad, of right and wrong, then the ground of the heart becomes as cultivated ground, just as the land does after ploughing. All the old stumps and roots and pebbles and rocks are taken off and it is made into ground which is now ready for the sowing of the seed. If there are rocks and stones and bricks still scattered there, and still some of the old roots lying there, then it is difficult for the seed to be sown; the ground is not in the condition the farmer wishes it to be.

The next thing in the attainment of the inner life is to seek a spiritual guide, someone whom a man can absolutely trust and have every confidence in, someone to whom he can look up, and with whom he is in sympathy, which would culminate in what is called devotion. And once he has found someone in life whom he considers his guru, his murshid, his guide, then to give to him all confidence, so that not a thing is kept back. If there is something kept back then what is given might just as well be taken away, because everything must be done fully, either have confidence or not have confidence, either have trust or no trust. On this path of perfection all things must be done fully.

Now there are the particular ways of the guide, which depend upon his temperament and upon his discrimination in finding for everyone who is being guided a special way. He may lead them to their destination by the royal road, or through the streets and lanes, down to the sea or through the town, by land or by water, the way that to him seems the best under certain circumstances.

The third thing necessary to spiritual attainment is the receiving of knowledge. This being the knowledge of the inner world, it cannot be compared with the knowledge one has learned before. That is why it is necessary to unlearn the former. Man cannot adjust what he receives in this path to the ideas which he has held before; the two things cannot go together. Therefore, there are three stages of receiving knowledge which the one being guided has to go through. The first stage is the receiving of the knowledge, when he does nothing but receive. The next stage is the period after this, and that stage is the as-

similating of what has been learned. He thinks upon it, he ponders upon it, in order that it may remain in his mind. It is just
like eating food and then assimilating it. The third stage is the
reasoning it out by oneself. Man does not reason it out as soon
as he has received it; if he did, he would lose the whole thing.
Because it is like a person who has learned a and b and c at one
stage, and then would ask how about words that did not begin
with those letters. He would reason it out much sooner than he
ought, for he has not yet learned the other letters. There is a
time which must necessarily be given to receiving, as one gives
time to eating. While one is eating one does not run about in
the street in order to assimilate the food. After a person has
finished his dinner, he can do everything possible to help digest
it. Assimilating is clearly understanding, feeling, and memorizing knowledge within oneself; not only that, but waiting until
its benefit and its illumination come as a result of achievement.

This last stage then in the receiving of knowledge is reasoning, to reason it through, "Why was it like that? What benefit
has come to me from that? How can it be made practicable in
life? How can it benefit myself and others?" That is the third
stage. If these stages are confused then the whole process becomes confused, and one cannot get that benefit for which one
treads the spiritual path.

The fourth grade of attainment of the inner life is meditation. If one has unlearned all that one has learned, if one has a
teacher, and if one has received the knowledge of the inner life,
still meditation is one thing which is most necessary, which in
Sufi terms is called *ryazat*. In the first place meditation is done
mechanically, at an hour which one has fixed upon as the hour
for devotion or concentration. The next step is to think of that
idea of meditation at other times during the day. And the third
stage is continuing meditation throughout day and night. Then
one has attained to the right meditation. If a person practices
meditation only for fifteen minutes in the evening and then

forgets altogether about it all day, he does the same thing as going to church on Sunday and the other days of the week forgetting all about it.

Intellectual training no doubt has its use in the achievement of the inner life, but the principal thing is meditation. That is the real training. The study of one year and the meditation of one day are equal. By this meditation I mean the right kind of meditation. If a person closes his eyes and sits doing nothing he may just as well go to sleep. Meditation is not only an exercise to be practiced. In meditation the soul is charged with new light and life, with inspiration and vigor; in meditation there is every kind of blessing. Some become tired of meditation, but that does not mean that they meditate; they become tired before having arrived at a stage where they really experience the effect of meditation. It is like those who become weary of practicing the violin; they are tired because they have not yet played the violin. Once they played they would never be weary. The difficulty is playing the violin and the difficulty is having patience with one's own playing.

Patience is required in meditation; why a person gets tired is because he is accustomed to activity throughout the day. His nerves are all inclined to go on and on in that activity, which is not really for his benefit, and yet it is giving him the inclination to go on; and when he sits with his eyes closed he feels uncomfortable, for the mind which has been active all day becomes restive, just like a horse after having had a long run. Then if you want that horse to stand still, it is restive. It cannot stand still, because every nerve has been active, and it becomes almost impossible to keep that horse still.

And so it is with man. Once I was with a man who was in the habit of meditating. While we were sitting near the fire and talking about things he went into silence, and I had to sit quiet until he opened his eyes. I asked him, "It is beautiful, is it not?" and he said, "It is never enough." For those who experience the joy of meditation there is nothing in this world which is more interesting and enjoyable. They experience the inner peace and the joy that cannot be explained in words, they touch perfection, or the spirit of light, of life, and of love,—all is there.

The fifth necessity in the spiritual path is the living of the everyday life. There are not strict morals which a spiritual guide enforces upon a person, for that work has been given to the outward religions. It is the exoteric side of spiritual work to which the outer morals belong, but the essence of morals is practiced by those treading the spiritual path. Their first moral is constantly to avoid hurting the feeling of another. The second moral principle is to avoid allowing themselves to be affected by the constantly jarring influences which every soul has to meet in life. The third principle is to keep balance under all different situations and conditions which upset this tranquil state of mind. The fourth principle is to love unceasingly all those who deserve love, and to give to the undeserving their forgiveness, and this is continually practiced by them. The fifth principle is detachment amidst the crowd, but by detachment I do not mean separation. By detachment is only meant rising above those bondages which bind man and keep him back from his journey toward the goal.

IX

The Angel-Man

THE HINDU WORD *deva* denotes an angel-man, and the Sufi term for this is *farishta khaslat*. Every soul has as its first expression angelic life, and therefore it is not surprising if man shows angelic traits in his life, for it is in the depth of his soul.

The soul coming through different spheres and planes of existence partakes of different attributes, and the attributes of the lower world become so collected and gathered around the soul that it almost forgets its very first experience of itself, its purest being. The soul that through all the worldly experiences has a tendency to turn toward its origin, its angelic state, shows a different character from the general characteristics of human beings. This soul shows the tendency of the compass that always points in a certain direction, whichever way it is moved or turned. And it is the same with a soul whose nature it is to be pointing to the origin and source from which every soul comes.

Now this soul may have the same tendency from childhood and through youth, and when grown-up it may still have the same tendency; it may develop it more and more, but it is a tendency which is born with the soul and its magnetism is great. It attracts every other soul, because it is in contact with its real self, and that is the real self of every soul which it contacts. Therefore it acts as a magnet toward these souls. *Deva* is the name of this pure kind of human soul.

The next type of soul to the *deva* is the *jinn*. This is a characteristic of a soul that keeps in contact with the inner region, which is reflected outwardly in all that is beautiful. While the soul of every person is looking for the beauty which is outward, the attention of the *jinn*-soul is directed not so much to that beauty which is reflected outwardly as it is to the source of that beauty, which is within.

It is among those who live the inner life that these two characteristic types of the *deva* or angel and the *jinn* are mostly to be found, because they are less absorbed in the life of this world, so more attracted to the inner life. It does not mean that they are not occupied with the worldly life; it does not mean that they take no interest in this world; in fact it is the interest in the external life which brings the soul toward it. If the soul were not interested in the world it would not come; it is its interest which brings it. But to such a soul, while the external life is of interest, at the same time it is a disappointment. All that interests a fine soul in this world only interests as long as it does not touch it; once it has touched it this soul loses interest in it, its natural inclination is to withdraw. The things which hold the average soul cannot hold this soul; they can only attract, for this soul is seeking for something and sees the reflection of that outwardly. But when the soul touches it, it finds it was a shadow and not real, and it goes back disappointed. The life of the *deva* or *jinn* is spent in this manner.

The characteristic of the deer as described by the poets of India is that when it is thirsty it runs about in the forests looking for water. It is greatly delighted on hearing the sound of thunder, and runs about with a desire to drink; but sometimes there is only thunder and no rain afterwards, or if its rains it is perhaps only a shower and not enough to drink and the deer still remains thirsty. So is the thirst of a fine soul in this world. The soul of the spiritually inclined man is constantly thirsty, looking for something, seeking for something; and when it thinks it has found, the thing turns out to be different and so life becomes a continual struggle and disappointment. The result is that instead of taking interest in all things, a kind of indifference is produced, and yet in the real character of this soul there is no indifference, there is only love.

Although life seems to make this soul indifferent, it cannot really become indifferent, and it is this state working through this life that gives man a certain feeling, to which only a Hindu word is applicable; no other language has a word which can give you this particular meaning so adequately. The Hindus call it *vairagya* from which the term *vairagi* has come. *Vairagi* means a person who has become indifferent; and yet indifference is not the word for it. It describes a person who has lost the value in his eyes of all that attracts the human being. It is no more attractive to him; it no more enslaves him. He may still be interested in all things of this life, but is not bound to them. The first feeling of the *vairagi* is to turn away from everything. That person shows the nature of the deer, which runs away at the flutter of a leaf, for the person becomes sensitive and convinced of the disappointing results that come from the limitation and changeableness of life in the world. Hurt within, he becomes sensitive, and the first thing that occurs to his mind is to fly, to hide somewhere, to go into a cave in the mountains, or into the forest where he will meet no one. No affair of this world, no relation, no friendship, no wealth, no rank or position or comfort, nothing holds him. And yet that does not mean that he in any way lacks what is called love or kindness, for if ever he lives in this world it is only out of love. While he is not interested in the world it is only love that keeps him here, the love which does not express itself any more in the way of attachment, but only in the way of kindness, forgiveness, generosity, service, consideration, sympathy, helpfulness, in any way that it can. He is never expecting a return from the world, but ever doing all he can, pitying the conditions, knowing the limitedness of life and its continual changeability.

When this *vairagi* becomes more developed, then he becomes like a serpent. He becomes wise like a serpent. He seeks solitude as the serpent seeks solitude. The serpent is never interested in moving among the crowd; it always has its hole where it hides itself; it only comes out when it is hungry or thirsty, and once it has taken its food it does not hunger or thirst after more as the dogs and cats do; you can give them food again and again, and they still want more. Once the serpent is fed it goes into its hole and stays there until it wants food again; it has lost all voracity.

And so has the soul of the *vairagi*; he only wants to live in this world for the sake of others, not for himself. His connection with people in the world is to serve them, not asking for their service; to love them, not asking for love; to be friends with them, not asking for friendship. He never allows himself to be deceived a second time, once disappointed is sufficient. Once the *vairagi* has come to realize the falsehood of ordinary life he never allows himself to be deceived again. He sees the world with the eye of experience, and he says, "I do not expect anything from you; if I come to you it is to give to you, not to take from you; I do all things for you, but will not be bound to you." That is the watchword of the *vairagi*.

When the *vairagi* is still more developed in this feeling of *vairagya* then he becomes a lion. He is no more the serpent seeking solitude, although he loves it still; he is no more the deer, running away from the crowd. He is the lion, who stands and faces all difficulties. No longer sensitive, but with all strength and power, with all balance, with patience he endures, and with a brave spirit he stands in the crowd in the world. For what? To bear all things that come to him; to endure all the jarring influences that the world offers to a sensitive person; to look into the eyes of all, being brave in spirit and strengthened in truth and clear of conscience.

It is in this way that the lion-like soul of the *deva*, the angel-man, comes to the rescue of humanity. What is called the master or the saint, or prophet or sage is this developed *vairagi*. He is like the fruit that has ripened on the tree, helped by the sun. In this way this soul that is ripened by experience in life, and has not allowed itself to become decayed by that experience but has upheld the truth, with balance, with hope and patience, directed by love for humanity and desire to serve God, without any desire for appreciation or return from below or from above—this soul of the *deva* brings the divine Message, whenever the Message comes, to a community, a nation, or to the world.

X

Five Different Kinds of Spiritual Souls

THOSE WHO LIVE THE INNER LIFE have to adopt a certain outer form of living in the world amidst people of all kinds. There are five principal ways known which the spiritual souls adopt to meet life in the world, although there are many more ways. Very often they are found in such forms of life that one could never imagine for one moment that they were living the inner life. It is for this reason that the wise of all ages have taught respect for every human being—whatever be the outward character of that person—and have advised man to think who is behind that garb and what it is.

Among the five principal characteristics of the spiritual being, the first is the religious character. This is a person who lives the religious life, the life of an orthodox, like everybody else, not showing any outward trace of a deeper knowledge or wider view, though he realizes it within himself. Outwardly he goes to his religious temple, or his church, the same as everybody else. He offers his prayers to the Deity in the same form as everybody, reads the Scriptures in the same way that everybody else does, receives the sacraments and asks for the benediction of the church in the same way that everybody does. He shows no difference, no special characteristics outwardly showing him to be spiritually advanced; but at the same time while others are doing all their religious actions outwardly, he realizes them in his life in reality. Every religious action to him is a symbolical revelation; prayer to him is a meditation; the Scripture to him is his reminder, for the Holy Book refers him to that which he reads in life and in nature. Therefore while outwardly he is only a religious man like everybody in the world, inwardly he is a spiritual man.

Another aspect of a spiritual man is to be found in the philosophical mind. He may show no trace at all of orthodoxy or piety; he may seem to be quite a man of the world in business, or in the affairs of the worldly life. He takes all things smoothly, he tolerates all things, endures all things. He takes life easily with his understanding. He understands all things inwardly; outwardly he acts according to life's demand. No one may ever think that he is living the inner life. He may be settling a business affair, and yet he may have the realization of God and truth at the same time. He may not appear at all meditative or contemplative, and yet every moment of his life may be devoted to contemplation. He may take his occupation in everyday life as a means of spiritual realization. No one outwardly may consider for one moment that he is spiritually so highly evolved, except that those who come in contact with him may in time be convinced that he is an honest person, that he is fair and just in his principles and life, that he is sincere. That is all the religion he needs. In this way his outward life becomes his religion, and his inner realization his spirituality.

The third form of a spiritual being is that of a server, one who does good to others. In this form there may be saints hidden. They never speak about spirituality, nor much about the philosophy of life. Their philosophy and religion are in their action. There is love gushing forth from their heart every moment of their life, and they are occupied in doing good to others. They consider everyone who comes near them as their brother or sister, as their child, and take an interest in their joy and their sorrow. They do all they can to guide them, to instruct them, to advise them through their life. In this form the spiritual person may be a teacher, a preacher or a philanthropist, but in whatever form he may appear, the chief thing in his life is the service of mankind, doing good to another, bringing happiness to someone in some form; and the joy that rises from this is high spiritual ecstasy, for every act of goodness and kindness has a particular joy which brings the air of heaven. When all the time a person is occupied doing good to others, there is a constant joy arising, and that joy creates a heavenly atmosphere, creating within him that heaven which is his inner life. This world is so full of thorns, so full of troubles, pains, and sorrows, and in this same world he lives; but by the very fact of his trying to remove the thorns from the path of another, although they prick his own hands, he rises, and this gives him that inner joy which is his spiritual realization.

There is the fourth form of a spiritual person, which is the mystic form, and that form is difficult to understand, because the mystic is born. Mysticism is not a thing which is learned, it is a temperament. A mystic may have his face turned toward the north while he is looking toward the south; a mystic may have his head bent low and yet he may be looking up; his eyes may be open outwardly while he may be looking inwardly; his eyes may be closed and yet he may be looking outwardly. The average man cannot understand the mystic, and therefore people are always at a loss when dealing with him. His "yes" is not the same yes that everybody says; his "no" has not the same meaning as that which everybody understands. In almost every phrase he says there is some symbolical meaning. His every outward action has an inner significance. A man who does not understand his symbolical meaning may be bewildered by hearing a phrase which is nothing but confusion to him.

A mystic may take one step outwardly, inwardly he has taken a thousand; he may be in one city and may be working in another place at the same time. A mystic is a phenomenon in himself and a confusion to those around him. He himself cannot tell them what he is doing, nor will they understand the real secret of the mystic, for it is someone who is living the inner life and at the same time covering that inner life by outer action;

his word or movement is nothing but the cover of some inner action. Therefore those who understand the mystic never dispute with him. When he says "go" they go; when he says "come" they come; when he comes to them they do not say "do not come," they understand that it is the time when he must come; and when he goes from them they do not ask him to stay, for they know it is the time when he must go.

Neither the laughter of a mystic nor his tears are to be taken as any outward expression which means something. His tears may perhaps be a cover for very great joy, his smile, his laughter, may be a cover for a very deep sentiment. His open eyes, his closed eyes, the turning of his face, his glance, his silence, his conversation, nothing means the same that one is accustomed to understand. Yet it does not mean that the mystic does this purposely, he is made thus; no one could purposely do it even if he wished, no one has the power to do it. The truth is that the soul of the mystic is a dancing soul. It has realized that inner law, it has fathomed that mystery for which souls long, and in the joy of that mystery the whole life of the mystic becomes a mystery. You may see the mystic twenty times a day and twenty times he will have a different expression. Every time his mood is different, and yet his outward mood may not at all be his inner mood. The mystic is an example of God's mystery in the form of man.

The fifth form in which a person who lives the inner life appears is a strange form, a form which very few people can understand. He puts on the mask of innocence outwardly to such an extent that those who do not understand may easily consider him unbalanced, peculiar, or strange. He does not mind about it for the reason that it is only his shield. If he were to admit before humanity the power that he has, thousands of people would go after him and he would not have one moment to live his inner life. The enormous power that he possesses governs inwardly lands and countries, controlling them and keeping them safe from disasters, such as floods and plagues and also wars, keeping harmony in the country or in the place in which he lives, and all this is done by his silence, by his constant realization of the inner life. To a person who lacks deep insight he will seem a strange being. In the language of the East he is called *Madzub*. That same idea was known to the ancient Greeks and the traces of it are still in existence in some places, but mostly in the East. There are souls to be found today in the East, living in this garb of a self-realized man who shows no trace outwardly of philosophy or mysticism or religion, or any particular morals; yet his presence is a battery of power, his glance most inspiring, a commanding expression in his looks; and if he ever speaks, his word is the promise of God. What he says is Truth, but he rarely speaks a word, it is difficult to get a word out of him; but once he has spoken, what he says is done.

There is no end to the variety of the outward appearance of spiritual souls in life, but at the same time there is no better way of living in this world and yet living the inner life than being *one's self*, outwardly and inwardly. Whatever be one's profession, work, or part in the outer life, to perform it sincerely and truthfully, to fulfil one's mission in the outer life thoroughly, at the same time keeping the inner realization that the outer life, whatever be one's occupation, should reflect the inner realization of truth.

SUFI MYSTICISM

I

Mysticism

MYSTICISM IS THE ESSENCE of all knowledge, science, art, philosophy, religion, and literature. These all come under the heading of mysticism, for mysticism is the basis of all knowledge.

When one traces the origin of medicine, which has developed into the pure science it is today, one will find that its source was in intuition. It is the mystics who have given it to the world. For instance Avicenna, the great Persian mystic, has contributed more to medicine than any other man in the world history of medicine. We know the meaning of science to be a clear knowledge based on reason and logic; but at the same time, where did it start? Was it by reason and logic? First there was intuition, then came reason, and finally logic was applied to it. Furthermore, in the lower creation there are no doctors, yet the creatures are their own physicians. The animals know whether they will best be cured by standing in the sun, by bathing in a pool of water, by running in the free air, or by sitting quietly under the shade of a tree. I once knew a sensible dog who used to fast every Thursday. No doubt many people of the East would say he was an incarnation of a Brahmin, but to me it was a puzzle how the dog knew it was Thursday!

People think a mystic means a dreamer, an unpractical person who has no knowledge of worldly affairs. But such a mystic I would call only half a mystic. A mystic in the full sense of the word must have balance; he must be as wise in worldly matters as in spiritual things. People have had many misconceptions of what a mystic is. They have called a fortune-teller a mystic, or a medium, a clairvoyant, a visionary. I do not mean that a mystic

does not possess all these qualities, but these qualities do not
make a mystic. A real mystic should prove to be an inspired
artist, a wonderful scientist, a powerful statesman. He should
have just as good qualifications for business, for industry, for
social and political life, as the materially minded man. When
people say to me, "You are a mystic, I thought you would take
no notice of this or that," I do not like it. Why should I not take
notice of it? I take notice of every little detail, although every
little detail does not occupy my mind so much that I take notice
of nothing else. It is not necessary to be unconscious of the
world while being conscious of God. With our two eyes we see
one vision; so we see both aspects, God and the world, as a clear
vision at the same time. It is difficult, but not impossible.

Mysticism is an outlook on life. Things which seem real to
an average person are unreal in the eyes of the mystic; and the
things that seem unreal in the eyes of the average person are
real in the eyes of the mystic.

For the mystic God is the source and goal of all. God is all,
and all is God; but a real mystic does not say, as an intellectual
student of philosophy does, "I do not believe in God, but I
believe in the abstract." Such a man is unpoetic and without an
ideal. He may have got hold of some truth, but it is a flower
without fragrance. One cannot worship the abstract; no one can
communicate with the abstract, give anything to it, nor take
anything from it. To worship in that way is meaningless. We
must have something before us to love, to worship, to adhere
to, to look up to, to raise high. But while it is true if we say,
"God is everything and all," yet at the same time, from another
point of view, "everything" means "nothing."

The mystic says, "If you have no God, make one." It is the
man without an ideal and without imagination who ignores
God. A cup of water is as interesting as the ocean, or perhaps
even more so when one is thirsty. A personal God is as important as, or even more important than, the idea of the abstract

from which we gain nothing. We human beings have our limited mind. We can grasp the idea of God inasmuch as we can conceive of God. For instance we may have a friend whom we love and whom we wish to praise; and yet he is above our praise. All we can do is to say, "How kind, how good, how patient, or how wonderful is my friend." That is all. Our words cannot make him greater. Our words cannot even express fully what we ourselves think of him. All we can do is to make a conception of our friend for our own understanding.

It is the same with God. Man cannot comprehend God fully. All he can do is to form a conception of God for himself in order to make comprehensible something which is unlimited. That is why the mystic does not say, "My realization of God is higher than yours, therefore I keep away from you." I have seen a mystic walking in a religious procession with the peasants, singing hymns with them before an idol of stone. He himself was greater than the god in the procession and yet he was singing with the same reverence as everybody else. He never had any desire to show that his belief, his realization, was higher or greater than the realization of the others.

The idea of God as abstract is the intellectual conception of those who have studied philosophy; for the mystic He is a reality. The mystic does not think of God as abstract, but he knows God to be so. It is not a question of knowing, but of being. God for the mystic is the stepping stone to self-realization. He is the gate, He is the door, the entrance to the heavens. God, for the mystic, is a key with which to open the secret of life, the abode from whence he comes and to which he returns and where he finds himself at home.

Once a Western seeker of truth went to a sage in China and said to him, "I have come to learn from you what truth is." The sage said, "Many of your missionaries come to us here and teach your faith. Why do you come to me?" "Well," he said, "what they teach about is God. We know about God; but now I come to you to ask you about the mystery of life." The sage said, "If you know God, that is all there is to be known, there is nothing more. That is all the mystery there is."

There is the question of the mystic's conception of Christ. Do we not know that one person is better than another, and is it not true that God is in man? If that is true, the mystic says, what objection is there if one person calls Christ God, and if the other believes Christ to be man? If God is in man, then if Christ is called God, what does it matter? And if Christ is called man, it only raises man, whom God has created, to that stature. Both have their reasons, and both are right, and yet they oppose one another. Some object to Christ being called divine; but if divinity is not sought in man, then in what shall we seek God? Can divinity be found in the tree, in the plant, in the stone? Yes indeed, God is in all; but at the same time it is in man that divinity is awakened, that God is awakened, that God can be seen.

The tolerance of the mystic is different. The people of a certain nation, race, or religion may say, "In Jesus Christ we see the Lord." Under that name they recognize their ideal. People of other countries have seen their divine ideal in Buddha. For their consolation and in support of their ideal they can all find in history the name of someone who has once existed. The Muslim says that Muhammad is the object of his worship, the Hindu says Krishna. As long as they have not realized the spirit of their ideal they will dispute, quarrel, and fight; and they will say, "My teacher is great," "Mine is greater still." But they do not see that it is one and the same spirit, manifesting in greater excellence. We exalt the teacher to the extent that we have understood him, but we do not exalt him enough if we call him by a certain name and thus limit him to a certain part of the world. But when we see the unlimited, we can call him by all names and say, "You are Krishna, you are Christ, and you are Buddha," just as the loving mother can call her child "my prince." She can give the most beautiful names to her child.

Once four little girls were disputing. One said, "My mother is better than yours." The second girl said, "My mother is better than your mother." So they were arguing and being quite disagreeable to one another. But someone who was passing by said to them, "It is not your mother or their mother, it is *the* mother who is always the best. It is the mother quality, her love and affection for her children." This is the point of view of the mystic in regard to the divine ideal.

The moral principle of the mystic is the love principle. He says, "The greater your love, the greater your moral. If we are forced to be virtuous according to a certain principle, a certain regulation, certain laws or rules, that is not real virtue. It must come from the depths of our heart; our own heart must teach us the true moral." Thus the mystic leaves morality to the deepening of the heart quality. The mystic says that the more loving someone's heart is, the greater is his morality.

There is no greater teacher of morals than love itself, for the first lesson that one learns from love is: I am not, you are. This is self-denial, self-abnegation, without which we cannot take the first step in love's path. One may claim to be a great lover, to be a great admirer, to be very affectionate, but it all means nothing; as long as the thought of self is there, there is no love. But when the thought of self is removed then every action, every deed that one performs in life, becomes a virtue. It cannot be otherwise. A loving person cannot be unjust, a loving person cannot be cruel. Even if what he does seems wrong in the eyes of a thousand people it cannot be wrong in reality. In reality it will be right, for it is inspired by love.

What is religion to the mystic? The religion of the mystic is a steady progress towards unity. How does he make this progress? In two ways. In the first way he sees himself in others, in the good, in the bad, in all; and thus he expands the horizon of his vision. This study goes on throughout his lifetime, and as he progresses he comes closer to the oneness of all things. And the other way of developing is to become conscious of one's own self in God, and of God in one's self, which means deepening the consciousness of our innermost being. This process takes place in two directions: outwardly by being one with all we see, and inwardly by being in touch with that one Life which is everlasting, by dissolving into it, and by being conscious of that one Spirit being *the* existence, the only existence.

The law of the mystic is the understanding of the law. The average man says, "This person has got the better of me. I will show him!" The mystic's outlook is different; he believes that no one can get away with anything in this world without paying for it. For every gain, the food one eats, every drop one drinks, every breath of air one takes, there is a tax to be paid. One is continually paying, and yet one does not know it. This shows that behind it all there is a perfect justice working. One cannot get the slightest comfort and pleasure without having to pay for it, and every pain has its own reward, though few seem to realize this. Therefore behind all this falsehood and injustice we see that there is a perfect wisdom working continually day and night. The mystic sees it in everything with open eyes; and that is the great phenomenon. For in the first place the mystical life is a puzzle, in the second place a bewilderment, and in the third place life is a phenomenon.

It is a puzzle when the law is not understood, a very interesting puzzle. There is no better game than to be occupied with that puzzle, to try and understand it, to solve it. It is so interesting that there is no sport or game that can be compared with it. Then it is a bewilderment, because of the difference between the way everybody looks at life and how it is in reality. There comes a stage when a person says, "Either they are all mad, or I am mad; but someone must be mad!"

The mystic can see from the point of view of everyone else

as well as from his own, which may be quite the contrary. For instance, in his teachings Christ says, "If anyone asks you for your coat, give him your overcoat also." A worldly man will say, "It is not practical; if someone asked this of me every day I would be continually buying new coats!" Yet at the same time it is more than practical from the point of view of the Master, for according to his view we cannot give anything, in whatever form, without getting it back in some way or other. Pure thought, good will, our service, our time, whatever we give, is never lost. It comes back to us according to our willingness to give; it comes back to us a thousandfold. That is why one is never the loser by being generous; one only gains.

The mystic sees the law working in all things and this gives him an insight into life. He begins to see why this misery has come upon him, why that pleasure has come; why one person is prospering and another not, why one is progressing and not the other. All these things become clear to him because he sees the law working in all things. The law of the mystic is not the law of the people. It is the law of nature; it is the real law.

A mystic never restricts himself to a certain rule, for instance to the rule of celibacy, although for certain experiences celibacy is of great importance. But if it is necessary for him to fast, practice celibacy, live on a vegetarian diet, or stay in a remote place in seclusion, or any other such thing, he can prescribe it for himself and be benefited by it. But one cannot say a mystic *must* do this or that, or that he must live a certain life; Solomon with his kingdom and all his grandeur was as great a mystic and as wise a man as many hermits in the forest. One cannot judge a mystic by his appearance. If he is a real mystic, he will be a king whether he is in the midst of the treasures of a court or sitting clad in a ragged mantle. He is a king just the same wherever he is. Neither money, a court, nor life in the world can take him away from mysticism. If he chooses to live in solitude, it is his fancy. If he wishes to be in the crowd, he may just as well be there. Whether a person sits in a remote place in the forest or in a baker's shop, if he is thinking of a high ideal his surroundings cannot touch him; he does not see them. There is no aspect of life that can deprive a mystic of his mystical spirit. He may be rich or poor, in the midst of the world or away from everything, he is a mystic just the same.

The way to perfection for the mystic is by the annihilation of the false ego. He understands that in man there is a real ego, that this ego is divine, but that the divine ego is covered by a false ego; and every man has a false ego because it begins to grow from his birth.

Man develops in himself a false idea, and that false idea is identification with something which he calls himself. He says, "I am a professor, a lawyer, a barrister, a doctor," or, "I am a king, a lord, or something." But whatever he claims, he is not that. His claim may be humble or proud, but in reality he is not that.

The mystic on the spiritual path perseveres in wiping out this false ego as much as he can, by meditation, by concentration, by prayer, by study, by everything he does. His one aim is to wipe out so much that one day reality, which is always there buried under the false ego, may manifest. And by calling on the name of God, by repeating the name of God everywhere, in the form or prayer, or in Zikr, or in any other form, what the mystic does is to awaken the spirit of the real ego in order that it may manifest just like a spring which rises out of a rock or a mountain. As soon as the water has gained power and strength, it breaks even through stone and rises as a stream. So it is with the divine spark in man. Through concentration, through meditation, it breaks out and manifests; and where it manifests it washes away the stains of the false ego and becomes a greater and greater stream, which becomes the source of comfort, consolation, healing, and happiness for all who come into contact with that spirit.

II

The Mystic

M YSTICISM IS NEITHER A FAITH nor a belief, nor is it a
principle or a dogma. A mystic is born; being a mystic
means having a certain temperament, a certain outlook on life.
It is for this reason that many are confused by the word *mystic,*
because mysticism cannot be explained in plain words.

To a mystic, impulse has divine significance. In every impulse a mystic sees the divine direction. What people call free
will is something that does not exist for a mystic. He sees one
plan, working and making its way toward a desired result, and
every person, whether willingly or unwillingly, contributes
towards the accomplishment of that plan; and this contribution
to the plan is considered by one to be free will and by another
accident. The one who feels, "This is my impulse; this is my
idea; this I must bring into action," only knows of the idea from
the moment it has become manifest to his view. He therefore
calls it free will. But from whence did that idea come to him?
Where does impulse come from? It comes, directly or indirectly,
from within. Sometimes it may seem to come from outside, but
it always starts from within, and thus every impulse for a mystic
is a divine impulse. One may ask, why is not every impulse
divine for everybody, since every impulse has its origin within?
It is because not everybody knows it to be so. The divine part
of the impulse is in realizing it is divine. The moment we are
conscious of the divine origin of the impulse, from that moment
it is divine. Although all through life it has come from within,
it is the fact of knowing this which makes it divine.

A mystic removes the barrier that stands between himself and another person by trying to look at life, not only from his own point of view, but also from the point of view of another. All disputes and disagreements arise from people's misunderstanding of each other, and mostly people misunderstand each other because they have their fixed point of view and are not willing to move from it. This is a rigid condition of mind. The more dense a person, the more he is fixed in his own point of view. Therefore it is easy to change the mind of an intelligent person, but it is most difficult to change the mind of a foolish person once it is fixed. It is the dense quality of mind which becomes fixed in a certain idea, and that covers the eyes so that they cannot see from the point of view of another person.

Many fear that by looking at things from the point of view of someone else they lose their own point of view, but I would rather lose my point of view if it was a wrong one. Why must one stick to one's point of view simply because it is one's own? And why should it be one's own point of view and not all points of view, the point of view of one and the same Spirit? For just as two eyes are needed to make the sight complete and two ears are necessary to make the hearing complete, so it is the understanding of two points of view, the opposite points of view, which gives a fuller insight into life.

A mystic calls this unlearning. What we call learning is fixing ideas in our mind. This learning is not freeing the soul; it is limiting the soul. By this I do not mean to say that learning has no place in life, but only that learning is not all that is needed in the spiritual path; there is something besides, there is something beyond learning, and to this we can only attain by unlearning. Learning is just like making knots of ideas, and the thread is not smooth as long as the knots are there. They must be unravelled, and when the thread is smooth one can treat it in any way one likes. A mind with knots cannot have a smooth circulation of truth; the ideas which are fixed in one's mind block it. A mystic, therefore, is willing to see from all points of view in order to clarify his knowledge. It is that willingness which is called unlearning.

The sense of understanding is one and the same in all of us, and if we are willing to understand, then understanding is within our reach. Very often we are not willing to understand, and that is why we do not understand. Mankind suffers from a sort of stubbornness. A man goes against what he thinks comes from another person. And yet everything he has learned has come from others; he has not learned one word from himself. All the same he calls it his argument, his idea, and his view, although it is no such thing; he has always taken it from somewhere. It is by accepting this fact that a mystic understands all, and it is this which makes him a friend of all.

A mystic does not look at reasons as everybody else does, because he sees that the first reason that comes to his mind is only a cover over another reason which is hidden behind it. He has patience, therefore, to wait until he has lifted the veil from the first reason, until he sees the reason behind it. Then again he sees that this reason which was hidden behind the first reason is more powerful, but that there is a still greater reason behind it. And so he goes from one reason to another, and sees in reason nothing but a veil to cover reality. And as he goes further, penetrating the several veils of reason, he reaches the essence of reason. By touching the essence he sees the reason in everything, good and bad.

Compare a mystic with an average person who argues and disputes and fights and quarrels over the first reason, which is nothing but a cover. Compare the two. The one is ready to form an opinion, to praise and to condemn; while the other patiently waits until reality gradually unfolds itself. A mystic believes in the unknown and unseen, not only in the form of God, but the unknown that is to come, the unseen that is not yet seen; whereas the other has no patience to wait until he knows the unknown, until he sees the unseen. A mystic does not urge the knowledge of the unknown or unseen upon another, but he sees the hand of the unknown working through all things. For instance, if a mystic has the impulse to go out and walk towards the north, he thinks there must be some purpose in it. He does not think it is only a whim, a foolish fancy, although the reason for it he does not know. But he will go to the north, and he will try to find the purpose of his going there in the result that comes from it.

The whole life of the mystic is mapped on this principle, and it is by this principle that he can arrive at the stage where his impulse becomes a voice from within that tells him "go here," "go there," or "leave," "move," or "stay." Therefore while others are prepared to explain why they are doing something or going somewhere or what they wish to do, the mystic cannot explain, because he himself does not know. And yet he knows more than the person who is ready to answer why he is going and what he is going to accomplish, for what does man know about what will happen to him? He makes his programme and plans, but he does not know.

Man proposes and God disposes. Many say this every day, yet at the same time they make their programmes and lay out their plans. A mystic is not particular about it. He is working on the plan which is laid out already and he knows that there is a plan. He may not know the plan in detail; but if anyone can and will know the plan, it is the mystic. This again tells us something: that the one who knows little, knows most; and those who seem to know more, know the least.

The outlook of the mystic is like that of a man standing on a mountaintop and looking at the world from a great height. And if a mystic looks upon everyone as being not much different one from another, because they are all like children to him, it is like what we see from the top of a mountain. All people whether tall or short seem to be of the same size; they appear like little beings moving about; and an average man is frightened of truth in the same way that a person who has never been on a great height gets frightened at the sight of the immensity of space. The truth is immense, and when a person reaches the top of understanding he becomes frightened and he does not want to look at it.

Many have told me, "Eastern philosophy interests us very much, but the conception of Nirvana is very frightening." And I have answered, "Yes, it is frightening for the one who is not accustomed. Truth is just the same: truth is also frightening, but truth is reality." Besides, man is so fond of illusion that he so to speak revels in it. If someone awakens a man who is having an interesting dream, that man will say, "Oh, let me sleep on!" He likes looking at his dream; he does not want to wake up to reality because reality is not as interesting as the dream. Thus among the seekers after truth we find only one in a thousand who is courageous enough to look at the immensity of truth. But there are many who take an interest in illusion, and they are inclined, out of curiosity, to look at mental illusions, because these are different from the illusion of the physical life. And they are apt to call this mysticism, but it is not mysticism. No one can be a mystic and call himself a Christian mystic, a Jewish mystic or a Mohammadan mystic. For what is mysticism? Mysticism is something which erases from one's mind all idea of separateness, and if a person claims to be this mystic or that mystic he is not a mystic; he is only playing with a name.

People say that a mystic is someone who dreams and who lives in the clouds; my answer to this is that the real mystic stands on earth, but his head is in heaven. It is not true that the wise man is not intellectual, or that the wise man is not clever. A clever man is not necessarily wise, but the one who has the higher knowledge has no difficulty in gaining knowledge of worldly things. It is the man who has knowledge of worldly things only who has great difficulty in absorbing the higher knowledge. Mr. Ford was very wise when he said to me, "If you had been a business man, I am sure you would have been successful." Furthermore, he said, "I have tried all my life to solve the problem which you appear to have solved." This again gives us an insight into the idea that higher wisdom does not debar a person from having worldly wisdom, though worldly wisdom does not qualify a person to attain to the higher wisdom.

And now let us come to the mystic's vision. People think that to see colors or spirits or visions is mystical. But mysticism cannot be restricted to this, and those who see these things are not necessarily mystics. Besides, those who can see and whose vision is clear, say so little about it. The mystic will be the last to claim that he sees or does wonderful things; his vision and his power would be diminished as soon as he began to feed his vanity by claiming to know or do things which others cannot know or do. The main thing that the mystic has to accomplish is to get rid of the false ego, so that if he feeds it on claiming such things he will lose all his power and virtue and greatness.

To a mystic every person is like an open letter, just as to an experienced physician a person's face tells his condition. And yet a mystic would never say to someone else, "In this person I see this or that," for the more he knows the greater trust is put in him by God. He covers all that should be covered; he only says what has to be said. A mystic will know most and yet will act innocently. It is the ones who know little who make a fuss about their knowledge. The more a person knows, the less he shows to others. Besides, a mystic is never ready to correct people for their follies, to condemn them for their errors, or to accuse them of foolishness. He sees so much of errors and follies and foolishness that he never feels inclined to point them out; he just sees life in its different aspects, and understands the process an individual goes through in life. It is by mistakes and errors that one learns in the end, and a mystic never feels that he should condemn anyone for them; he only feels that they are natural. Some are advancing rapidly, others are going slowly. Foolishness is just like light and darkness: it is through darkness that the sun rises, and through ignorance wisdom will rise one day. A mystic, therefore, need not learn patience; he is taught patience by life from the beginning till the end. A mystic need not learn tolerance; his outlook gives him tolerance, it is natural for him. He need not learn forgiveness; he cannot do anything but forgive.

Man loves complexity and calls it knowledge. A great many societies and institutions in the world which call themselves occult and esoteric and psychic and by various other names, knowing that everyone is interested in complexity, cover the truth; and instead of covering it with one cover they cover it with a thousand covers to make it more interesting. It is just like customs which were followed in ancient times when people came to worship and asked the priest how they should do it, and he would say, "How far do you live from the shrine?" And when they said, "Two miles," he answered, "You must come on foot to the shrine and walk around it a hundred times before you may enter it." He gave them a good exercise before they were allowed to come in. And even today they do the same thing. When a person says, "I want to see truth," but wishes to look for truth in complexity, they cover truth under a thousand covers and then they give him the problem to solve. Are there not many people interested in the mahatmas of the Himalayas, are there not many searching for holy souls in remote places of Persia, many who look for a master in the centre of Australia? Perhaps next year an article will appear declaring that a great soul has been found in Siberia. What is it all about? It is all the love of complexity, queer notions, strange ideas which do not lead souls any further. Therefore a mystic very often appears to be simple, because sincerity makes him feel inclined to express the truth in simple language and in simple ideas, and because people value complexity, they think that what he says is very simple and that it is something which they have always known, that it is nothing new. But, as Solomon said, there is nothing new under the sun.

Besides, truth belongs to the soul and the soul knows it, and as soon as the truth is spoken the soul recognizes it; it is not new, not foreign to it. If a person says, "This is something I already know," even if his soul has known it, it can never be repeated too often for him. The great saints of the East have repeated one phrase, for instance, "God is One," perhaps a million times in their lives. Should we believe that they were so foolish as not to be able to understand the meaning of it by saying it once? Why then do they repeat it a million times? The reason is that it is never enough. We live in the midst of illusion from morning till evening when we go to sleep. What we do not know is the illusion in which we are from morning till evening. It is not the truth we do not know; truth is all we know—if we know anything fully. The mystic, therefore, instead of learning truth, instead of looking for truth, wishes to maintain truth; he wishes to cling to the idea of truth, to keep the vision of reality before him lest it may be covered by the thousand veils of illusion.

Does the mystic make any effort to reach the highest realization? Yes. It is an art which is passed on from teacher to pupil, and so this art is handed down through the ages from one person to another. One might ask why, if truth is within oneself, is there any necessity for such an art. But, after all, art is not nature. The animals and birds do not need an art; they are happy, they are peaceful, they are innocent, they are spiritual, really spiritual. They live in nature, their life is natural. We live far away from nature, we have made our artificial world to live in; and that is why we require an art to free ourselves from it. I do not mean to say that we must abandon life, or that we must not have anything to do with life in order to be mystics, but we have to practise that art which enables us to get in touch with reality.

That art is in the first place concentration. Concentration does not mean closing the eyes and sitting in church on Sunday. Many know how to close their eyes and sit there, yet their mind wanders about, especially when they have closed their eyes. Concentration means that every atom of the body and of the mind is centred in one spot.

The next stage is contemplation; that is to be able to retain an idea which raises one's consciousness from the dense world. The third stage is meditation, and that is to purify oneself, to free oneself, and to open oneself to the light of truth, in order that it may abide in one's spirit. And the fourth step is realization. Then the mystic is no longer the knower of truth, but is truth itself.

III

Realization

THERE IS ONE GOD and one truth, one religion and one mysticism; call it Sufism or Christianity or Hinduism or Buddhism, whatever you wish. As God cannot be divided, so mysticism cannot be divided.

It is an error when a person says, "My religion is different from yours." He does not know what religion means. Neither can there be many mysticisms, just as there cannot be many wisdoms; there is one wisdom. It is an error of mankind to say: this is Eastern and that is Western; this only shows lack of wisdom.

It is the same divine truth that man inherits, no matter to

what part of the world he belongs. To distinguish between occultism and mysticism is also an error, just as it would be an
error to say of one's eyes: this is my eye and that is yours. The
two eyes belong to one soul. When a person pictures mysticism
as a branch of a tree which is truth, he is wrong in thinking it to
be a branch; for mysticism is the stem which unites all branches.
Mysticism is the way by which to realize the truth. Jesus Christ
said, "I am the truth and I am the way." He did not say, "I am
the truth and I am the ways"; for there is only one way. There
is another way which is the wrong way. Many religions there
are, but not many wisdoms. Many houses of the Lord for worship, but only one God. Many scriptures, but one truth. So there
are many methods, but one way.

The methods of gaining that way of realization are many,
but there are four principal ones: by the heart, by the head, by
action, by repose. A person must choose from among these four
different methods of developing himself and preparing himself
to journey on the way, the only way, which is called mysticism.
No religion can call it its own, but it is the way of all religions.
No church can say that it owns it, for it belongs to all churches.
No one can say that his is the only way. It is the same way as all
others have to go.

People have often imagined that a mystic means an ascetic,
that a mystic is someone who dreams, a person who lives in the
air, someone who does not dwell here on the earth, a person
who is not practical; or that a person who is an ascetic must be
a hermit. This is not the case. And very often people think of
the mystic as a peculiar sort of man, and if they meet someone
who is peculiar, they say that he must be a mystic! This is a
wrong conception, an exaggeration, for a real mystic must show
equilibrium, balance. He will have his head in the heavens and
his feet on the earth. The real mystic is as wide awake in this
world as in the other. A mystic is not someone who dreams. He
is wide awake; yet he is capable of dreaming when others are

not, and of keeping awake when the rest cannot do so. A mystic strikes the balance between two things: power and beauty. He does not sacrifice power for beauty, nor beauty for power. He possesses power and enjoys beauty.

There are no restrictions in the life of the mystic; everything there shows balance, reason, love, and harmony. The religion of the mystic is every religion, and yet he is above what people call their religion. In point of fact he *is* religion. The moral of all religions is reciprocity; to reciprocate all the kindness we receive from others, to do an act of kindness to others without wanting any appreciation or return for it, and to make every sacrifice, however great, for love, harmony, and beauty.

The God of the mystic is to be found in his own heart; the truth of the mystic is beyond words. People argue and debate about things of little importance, but mysticism is not to be discussed. People want to talk in order to know, and then they forget it all. Very often it is not the one who knows who talks so much, but the one who wants to know. The one who knows but does not discuss is the mystic. He knows that happiness is in his own heart; but to put this into words is like putting the ocean into a drop of water.

Yet there is a wine which the mystic drinks, and that wine is ecstasy. A wine so powerful that the presence of the mystic becomes wine for everyone who comes into his presence. This wine is the wine of the real sacrament, whose symbol is found in the church. What is it, where does it come from, what is it made of? It may be called a power, life, a strength which comes through the mystic, through the spheres which every man is attached to. By his attachment to these spheres the mystic drinks the wine which is the sustenance of the human soul, and that wine is ecstasy, the mystic's intoxication. That intoxication is the love which manifests in the human heart. What does it matter, once a mystic has drunk that wine, whether he is sitting among the rocks in the wilderness or in a palace? It is all the same. The palace does not deprive him of the mystic's pleasures, neither does the rock take them away. He has found the kingdom of God on earth, about which Jesus Christ has said, "Seek ye first the kingdom of God and all these things shall be added unto you."

People strive for many different things in this world and last of all they seek the spiritual path. And there are some indifferent ones who say, "There is a long life before us and when the time comes that I must awake I shall wake up." But the mystic knows that this is the one thing he must attend to, that all other things come after that. It is of the greatest importance in his life.

Should he, by working for realization of God, neglect his duties in the world? It is not necessary. There is nothing that a mystic need renounce in order to have the realization of life. He only needs to attach the greatest importance to what is most important in life.

The life of a mystic is meditative, but to him meditation is like the winding of a clock. It is wound for a moment, and all day long it goes by itself. He does not have to think about it all day long. He does not trouble about it.

A shah of Persia used to sit up at night for his vigils and prayers. And a friend who was visiting him wondered at his long meditations after the whole day's work. "It is too much," he said, "you do not need so much meditation." "Do not say so," was the answer, "you do not know. For at night I pursue God, and during the day God follows me." The moments of meditation set the whole mechanism in running order, like a stream running into the ocean. They do not in the least keep the mystic from his duty; they only bless every word he speaks with the thought of God.

In all he thinks or does there is the perfume of God, which becomes a healing and a blessing. And if one asks how a mystic, who has become so kind and helpful, gets on among the crowd in everyday life, since the rough edges of everyday life rubbing against him must necessarily make him heartsore, the answer is that they certainly do, and the heart of the mystic is even more sore than that of anybody else. Where there is only kindness and patience all the thorns will come. But just as the diamond by being cut becomes brilliant so does the heart; and when the heart has been sufficiently cut it becomes a flame which illuminates not only the life of the mystic, but also that of others.

IV

The Nature and Work of a Mystic

THERE IS A DIFFERENCE between a philosopher, a wise man, a mystic, and a sage. From a mystical point of view the philosopher is a person who knows the nature and character of things and beings, who has studied this, who has reasoned it out, and who understands it. A wise man is he who has been the pupil of life. Life has been his teacher; its sorrows and troubles and experiences have brought him to a certain understanding of life. A mystic, however, need not have had experience of life to teach him, nor the study of life to make him intellectual enough to understand it better. The mystic is born with the mystical temperament. His language is a different language, his experience a different experience; he so to speak communicates with life, with conditions, things, and beings. But the sage has all three of these qualities. The sage is a philosopher, a wise man, a mystic, all three combined.

It is possible that a mystic may be no philosopher; though the mystic always has a clear vision and understanding, he may not have the philosopher's means of expression. The difference is like that between short sight and long sight. The mystic may not see the outline of things distinctly, a philosopher may observe only the detail, while the wise man may not be a philosopher but has learnt wisdom from life, and he may be different from the mystic as well.

And yet, when they arrive at the stage of the culmination of knowledge, they all come closer together. For instance, I was once talking to a business man, a man who had spent nearly fifty years of his life in commerce, and had made a success of it. He had never believed in any religion, he had never studied any philosophy, except that sometimes he read the works of great poets. But after we had talked for about an hour on subjects concerning the inner life, he discovered that he was not very far from my own beliefs; that after all, the patience which is required to make money, the sacrifices one has to make in order to be successful, and the experiences one has to go through with those whom one works with daily in business had been for him both a practice and a study. And I found that he was not very far from the conclusions to which a wise man, a philosopher, a mystic, would come. It is he whom I would call a wise man, for by his wisdom he had reached that truth which is studied by the philosopher and which is attained by the mystic through meditation.

The meaning of philosophy has changed in modern times. People generally understand by philosophy that which one finds in the books written by European philosophers and which are read and studied at universities. But spiritual philosophy is different; it is a different kind of knowledge, an understanding of the origin, the nature, and character of things and beings. It necessitates the study of human nature, the study of conditions of life. It is the deeper insight into life which makes one a philosopher.

Mysticism is neither taught nor learned. A mystic is born; it is a temperament, it is a certain outlook on life, it is a certain attitude toward life that makes a man a mystic. His chief characteristic is that he knows the meaning of every action, whether it is by intuition or by accident, although to a mystic nothing is an accident. Every action, every condition, everything that happens, has a meaning and a purpose. Very often people find that a mystic has a queer temperament. He may suddenly think during the night, "I must go to the North," and in the morning he sets out on his journey; he does not know why, he does not know what he is to accomplish there, he only knows that he must go. By going there he finds something he has to do and sees that it was the hand of destiny pushing him toward the accomplishment of that purpose, which inspired him to go to the north. Or a mystic will tell a person to do or not to do a thing. If that person asks the reason he cannot tell him. His feeling comes by intuition, a knowledge which comes from the world unseen, and according to that knowledge he acts. Therefore the mystic's impulse is a divine impulse, and one can judge neither his action nor his attitude. One will find that there are various aspects of the mystic temperament.

But there is a knowledge which a mystic attains by means of the head and which prepares him to find his way to the truth. Reasoning is a faculty which the mystic uses, and which he may develop like any man of common sense, any practical man; the difference is only that the mystic does not stop at the first reason but wishes to see the reason behind all reasons. Thus in everything, whether right or wrong, the mystic seeks for the reason. The immediate answer, however, will be a reason which does not satisfy him, for he sees that behind that reason there is another reason. And so he progresses in the knowledge of all things, which is far greater than the knowledge gained by one thing. This is why neither wrong nor right, good nor evil, excites the mystic very much, neither does it greatly shock or surprise him. For everything seems to him to have its own nature, and it is understanding this which makes him feel at one with all that exists. And what can one wish for more in life than understanding? It is understanding that gives one harmony in the home with those near and dear to one, and peace outside the home with so many different natures and characters. If one lacks understanding one is poor, in spite of all that one may possess of the goods of this world, and it is understanding which gives a man riches.

If life could be pictured, one would say that it reminds one of the sea in a storm, the waves coming and going—such is life. And it is the understanding of this which gives man the weight which enables him to endure through rain and storm and all vicissitudes. Without understanding he is like a jolly-boat on the sea which cannot weather the storm. Through understanding a mystic learns. He learns tact; he is tactful under all circumstances; and his tact is like a heavily laden ship, which the wind cannot capsize and which rides steady in the midst of the storm.

The nature of life is such that it easily excites the mind and makes man unhappy in an instant. It makes man so confused that he does not know where to take the next step. In contrast with this the mystic stands still and inquires of life its secret; and from every experience, from every failure or success, the mystic learns a lesson; thus both failure and success are profitable to him.

The ideal of a mystic is never to think of disagreeable things. What one does not want to happen one should not think of. A mystic erases from his mind all the disagreeable things of the past. He collects and keeps his happy experiences, and out of them he makes a paradise. Are there not many unhappy people who keep part of the past before them, which causes them pain in their heart? Past is past; it is gone. There is eternity before us. If we want to make our life as we wish it to be, we should not think disagreeable thoughts and ponder over painful experiences and memories that make us unhappy.

It is for this reason that to some extent life becomes easy for a mystic to deal with. For he knows every heart, every nature, whereas those who are untouched by the mystic's secret suffer from their difficulties both at home and outside. They dread the presence of people they do not understand; they want to run away from them, and if they cannot escape they feel as if they are in the mouth of a dragon; and perhaps they are placed in a situation which cannot easily be changed. The consequence is that they heap confusion upon confusion. And how very often one sees that when two people do not understand one another, a third comes and helps them to do so, and the light thrown upon them causes greater harmony! The mystic says: whether it be agreeable or disagreeable, if you are in a certain situation, make the best of it; try to understand how to deal with such a situation. Therefore a life without such understanding is like a dark room which contains everything you wish: it is all there, but there is no light.

The world is after all a wonderful place, in spite of so many souls wishing to leave it. For there is nothing which cannot be obtained in this world; everything is there, all things good and beautiful, all things precious and worthwhile; they are all there, if only one knows their nature, their character, and how to obtain them.

If you ask some people what is the nature of life, they will say, "The further we go in striving for happiness, the further we are removed from it." This is true. But the one who does not know that unhappiness does not exist takes the wrong way. Besides, happiness is more natural than unhappiness, as good is more natural than evil, and health than illness. And yet man is so pessimistic. If we tell him how good someone is he cannot believe this to be true, but if we tell him how bad a person is he will readily believe it.

The work of a mystic, therefore, is to study life. To the mystic life is not a stage-play or an entertainment. For the mystic it is a school in which to learn, every moment of one's life; it is a continual study. And the scripture of the mystic is human nature; every morning he turns a new page of this scripture. And the books of the great ones who have brought the message to the world from time to time, and which became sacred scriptures and were read for thousands of years, generations of people taking their spiritual food from them, are the interpretations that they gave of this scripture which is human nature. That is why all the sacred scriptures always have the same sacred feeling.

The mystic respects all religions and he understands all the different and contradictory ideas, for he understands everyone's language. The mystic can agree, without having to dispute, with both the wise and the foolish. For he sees that the nature of facts is such that they are true in their own place; he understands every aspect of their nature. The mystic sees from every point of view. He sees from the point of view of each person and that is why he is harmonious with all. A man comes to a mystic and says, "I cannot believe in a personal God, it means nothing to me." Then the mystic answers, "You are quite right." Another man says, "The only way of making God intelligible is in the form of man." The mystic says, "You are right." And another person says, "How foolish of these people to make of this man a God; God is above comprehension." And the mystic will agree with him too. For a mystic understands the reason behind all the opposing arguments.

Once a missionary came to a Sufi in Persia, desiring to have a discussion and to prove his opinion on some Sufi teaching to be the right one. The Sufi was sitting there, in his silent, quiet attitude, with two or three of his pupils at his side. The missionary brought up some arguments, and the mystic answered, "You are right." Then the man went on to dispute but the Sufi only said, "That is quite true." The man was very disappointed as there was no opportunity for argument. The Sufi saw the truth in all.

The truth is like a piano: the notes may be high or low, one may strike a C or an E, but they are all notes. So the difference between ideas is like that between notes, and it is the same in daily life with the right and the wrong attitude. If we have the wrong attitude all things are wrong, if we have the right attitude all things are right. The man who mistrusts himself will mistrust his best friend; the man who trusts himself will trust everyone.

Things which seem to be apart, such as right and wrong, light and darkness, form and shadow, to the mystic appear so close that only a hair's breadth divides right and wrong. Before the mystic there opens an outlook on life, an outlook which discloses the purpose of life. The question which the mystic puts to himself is, "Which is my being? My body? No. This body is my possession. I cannot be that which I possess." He asks himself, "Is it my mind?" The answer comes, "No. The mind is something I possess, it is something I witness. There must be a difference between the knower and the known." By this method the Sufi comes to an understanding of the illusory character of all he possesses. It is like a man who has a coat made: it is his coat, it is not himself.

Then the mystic begins to think, "It is not myself that thinks, it is the mind. It is the body which suffers, it is not myself." It is a kind of liberation for him to know, "I am not my mind." For an ordinary man wonders why one moment he has a good thought, another moment a bad thought, one moment an earthly thought, the next moment a thought of heaven. Life for him is like a moving picture in which it is he who sees who is dancing there.

By seeing this the mystic liberates his real self, which owing to his illusion was buried under mind and body, what people call a lost soul, a soul which was not aware of the mystical truth that body and mind are the vehicles by which to experience life. And it is in this way that the mystic begins his journey toward immortality.

V

The Secret of the Spirit

THERE ARE FOUR DIFFERENT explanations of the word *spirit*.
One meaning is essence. Spirit of camphor means the essence of camphor. The second meaning of spirit is what is
understood by those who call the soul spirit when it has left the
body on earth and has passed to the other side. The third meaning of spirit is that of the soul and mind working together. It is
used in this sense when one says that a man seems to be in low
spirits; this means that both his mind and soul are depressed,
although one may not always define it in this way. And the
fourth meaning of spirit is the soul of all souls, the source and
goal of all things and all beings, from which all comes and to
which all returns.

The first meaning of the word spirit is, as I have said, essence.
The essence of flowers is honey, the essence of milk is butter,
the essence of grapes is wine, and the essence of learning is
wisdom. Therefore wisdom is as sweet as honey, as nourishing
as butter, and as exalting as wine.

To rise above things in life one must try to get to the essence.
In other words, there is one way of listening to a musician and
that is to consider the form, the technique; and the other way is
to grasp the feeling, the sense that the music suggests. So it is
with life; we can look at life in one way and see it in different
forms and make a rigid conception of it, or we can see it so that
we get the suggestion of its essence. For instance a person may
come to us and express a thousand false feelings. And then we
go over it in our mind and realize it was all false because it
could not reasonably be true; this is one way. The other way is

to see immediately that it is false from first to last, without going into details. This is quite sufficient, and because we have immediately seen it we have saved our mind a great deal of trouble.

Sometimes a person says to another, "You say you are my friend; all right, I am going to find out what you are like, how you work." That is one way of looking at it. But the other way is to look only once at that person and, by that one glance, to know what he is worth; that is all. If one can do this it will make one brave, venturesome, and will bring one nearer to the essence. It will impart generosity and liberality; otherwise one remains narrow and small and confused and in this way thousands and millions of souls are buffeted along on the sea of life, not knowing where they are going, because they are not sure of themselves. If a person says, "I don't know you, but perhaps I will know you some day," that person will never know anyone, for all his life he will be unsure.

As to the second meaning of the word spirit, this mechanism of the physical body, which works from morning till evening without winding like a machine, and which stands up to all the turmoil of life, encounters all difficulties, and endures everything that comes to it, one day falls flat; it is just like when the steam or electricity, or whatever it was that kept the machine going, suddenly seems to depart. A physician says that the man's heart failed, or his blood pressure was too high, or something like that as an explanation of death. It means that a person who was active and sensitive is no longer active nor sensitive. That which was most important in him has left. So much the physician can tell you; but what was there he does not know.

From the point of view of a mystic, however, what has left the body is the person. This body was not the person. This body was a mask which covered that person; and when this mask is cast off that person becomes invisible. Not he himself but only the mask has been thrown away. He is what he already was. If there is a death it is the removing of the mask.

A question arises: how does this take place; how does it happen? And the answer is that there is a magnetic action between the person and the mask. It is the strength of the physical body which holds the spirit, and it is the strength of the spirit which holds the body. The physical body holds on to the spirit because it only lives by the life of the spirit, and without the spirit it is dead. And as every being, however small, struggles for life, this physical body tries to hold on to the spirit; and it does so to the last, as someone who is on the point of losing his gold might hold it tightly in his hand until his hand is paralysed, and he can no longer hold it and so lets it drop. It does not mean he does not want it; it only means he cannot hold it any longer. And so it is with the spirit: as long as the spirit is interested in the physical body it holds it, permeates it, and embraces it. But as soon as it feels that it does not want it anymore, that it no longer has any use for the body, it drops it.

Both these tendencies can be seen in people when they are studied by those who understand. There are people who have reached old age and who are no longer doing anything in the world, yet each atom of their body is consciously or unconsciously holding on to the spirit in order to live every moment they can possibly prolong their life. And as long as their strength allows them to hold on to the spirit they live; and they may live to a very great age. But one can also notice another tendency, and that is that there are some who are tired of life. They no longer attach any importance to this life on earth. The value of things has diminished in their eyes; they are disappointed by these transitory and changeable conditions. In their spirit they are feeling something quite different. Their tendency is to give up the physical bondage of the body, and they would be glad if the spirit were separated from it; and yet their body unconsciously clings to the spirit just the same and keeps them alive as long as it can hold on. Thus the unwilling spirit is held by the body.

In conclusion, death means a separation from the body which is nothing but a garb covering the spirit. And what follows after the separation? The body which is left on the earth by the spirit is no longer living in the sense we understand life; yet it is living. It is as if there had been a fire in the stove, and even after the fire was extinguished the warmth remained there. There is only the smallest degree of spirit, but there is life in it. Where there is no life, life cannot be created; life must come out of life. Life cannot come out of death. Living creatures such as worms and germs come out of a dead body, and how could life come out if there were no life there? There is life; not in the sense we generally understand it, but it is living just the same. There is nothing in this world of which we can say that it is without life, or dead. Everything, every object that seems without life, has some life somewhere. And even after it is destroyed it is still living. When germs and worms manifest out of the dead body we think that it means it is finished. On the contrary it goes on, life is continued in various forms. It has never ended; what has ended is this imprisonment which we recognized as such and such a person; but the existence is still going on, even the moral existence, even the mask which in reality was nothing.

The living part was the spirit and it goes on living. When we say, "He has gone to the other world," the other world is our conception, though it is a beautiful conception. If one says, for instance, that a great revolution is taking place in the scientific world, it does not mean that the scientific world is outside this world. When we have experienced a great development in the mystical world, this does not mean that we live outside this planet. It is a conception; it is a beautiful way of putting it, and it is the best we can find. "In the other world" means in a world which is veiled from our eyes, our physical eyes; but it does not mean a world far away from us beyond our reach. Both the living and the dead inhabit the same space; we all live together. Only a veil separates us, the veil of this physical body. Separation means being unable to see one another; there is no other separation.

One need not attain to the seventh heaven in order to reach those who have passed. When one really cares for them, that bond of love and sympathy in itself makes us close to them. Two people may be living in the same house, working together, seeing each other every day, every hour, and yet they may be as far apart as the North Pole from the South Pole. There are people thrown miles apart by destiny so that they cannot reach one another because of life's difficult circumstances; and yet they can be closer to each other than anyone else. If this is true, it proves that those united in spirit may be thrown far apart in the world and yet be so close together that nothing stands between them. Therefore if those who have departed from this earth have a connection with someone on earth, they are close to him just the same. Nearness means nearness of the spirit, not of the physical body.

In India there used to be a custom called *sati*, by which a wife who was devoted to her husband was cremated with him. Some people felt great horror at the idea, but others thought differently. I would say in regard to this question that when two souls have become one, whether they are both on earth or whether one of them has gone to another plane, they are still united. If one of them remains living, then that living person is as though dead here, for he only lives there where there is real unity. There is no separation. Nothing can separate two souls if they are really united.

The third meaning of the spirit is that it is the mind and the soul together. One might ask if the mind and soul together, that is to say the spirit, is that part of one's being which lives. It is not a part, but all. Our overcoat is not a part of our being; it is something extraneous. It becomes temporarily a part, but it is not essentially a part. The real being is the spirit, the mind and the soul together.

One might think it uninteresting to live as spirit and not as body. It might seem uninteresting to one who has not experienced on this earth how to be able to live independently of the physical body. All mysticism has been based on this: how to be able to live independently of the physical body, how to live on earth as spirit, even for five minutes a day. This gives a conviction of being able to live and yet be independent of the physical body. It is an experience unlike any other experience in life, an education in the highest knowledge. Once a person has realized how he can exist without the physical body it produces a faith that gives an ultimate conviction which nothing can change.

It is not only a matter of existing, but of existing completely, fully. The soul is not dependent upon the eyes to see. It sees more than the physical eyes can see. It is not dependent upon the ears; it hears more than the ears can hear. Therefore he who knows spirit receives far greater inspiration from being able to exist independently of the physical body. It is very easy for a person with material knowledge to call those people fanatics who retire to the mountains or wander about thinking of spiritual things, who seem to live in a dream. They might appear to do so, but actually they only do not conform to what everyone else does. They left the life of business and profession and politics, all social life, for the sake of deeper experience. It is not necessary for everyone to follow their example, but one may benefit by what they have brought to us.

At this time West and East are coming closer together. What is needed now is that we should awaken and benefit by the fruits of the lives of people in both East and West. There is much that the West can give to the East. It has labored along certain lines, and the fruits of this work can be of use to the East, while there are fruits which Eastern people have gathered for years and years which will be of great use to the West once people have realized this. And the particular lesson which can be learned from the experience of those in the East who have investigated life's secret is the way of becoming conscious of one's spirit, of realizing spirit. No doubt those who wish to mystify others make complexities out of simple things. But those who wish to serve the world in the path of truth change complex things into simple ones. It is in a simple form that we have to realize the truth.

The fourth meaning of spirit is the source and the goal of all things; something toward which all are bound, to which all will return. It is that spirit which in religion is called God. And the best way of explaining this meaning of spirit is that it is like the sun, the center of all life, the divine spark in us. But the sun is not as small as it appears to be. Then what is the sun? The sun is all. The part of the sun that we recognize as the sun is the center of it, but the sun is in reality as large as its light reaches. The real sun is light itself. But as there is a point which is the central focus of light, we call that point the sun.

The light has centralized itself there; but the sun has other aspects such as rays, which are not different from the sun but which are the sun itself. And what are we? Our souls are the rays of the sun. In our inner being we are both source and goal itself. It is only our ignorance of this which keeps us ignorant of our own being.

Every atom of the universe, having come from the sun, from the divine sun, makes every effort to return to it. The tendency of the waves is to reach upward, of the mountains to point upward, of the birds to fly upward. The tendency of animals is to stand on their hind legs. The tendency of man is to stand upright, ready to soar upward. An angel is pictured as a man with two wings ready to fly upward. Science has discovered the law of gravitation, but the mystic knows the other law, which is also a law of gravitation but in the opposite direction.

Thus not only is every soul attracted in that direction, but also every atom of this world, going through all the different processes known to biology in order to reach that state, to return to the spirit. Therefore it is not necessary to be frightened by going toward God or by trying to attain the spirit to lose one's identity, one's individuality. A fear like this is the same as the experience of someone on the top of a mountain. A kind of terror overwhelms a person when he is looking at the immensity of the view; and in the same way a soul is frightened of spiritual attainment because of the immensity, of the largeness and depth it has. It frightens the soul which fears to lose itself, because it has this false conception of its smaller self. The mystic says, "Try to die before death," and to die before death is to play death; that means to get above this fright which only comes from the false conception of self.

The one who has died before death has no longer desire; he is above desire. This is shown by the picture of the god Vishnu sitting upon the lotus. The lotus represents desire: every petal is a desire. Sitting upon the lotus means that the desire is under him instead of being above his head. To some extent there is a relationship between life in the spiritual world and life on earth, for that which is collected here on earth indicates the task one has to perform here. The only condition is that the one who has stayed a shorter while here must work more for his spiritual accomplishment than the one who has stayed longer on earth. When someone has achieved spirituality here, it is not necessary for him to stay longer unless it is his desire.

The day the false conception of self is removed from one's eyes one begins to see the immensity of life. All that one sees is but one single vision of God's majesty.

VI

The Mystical Heart

WHEN ONE ASKS, "What is the heart? Where is the heart?" the answer usually is that the heart is in the breast. This is true; there is a nerve center in the breast of man which is so sensitive to our feelings that it is always regarded as the heart. When a person feels a great joy it is in that center that he feels something lighting up, and through the lighting up of that center his whole being seems light. He feels as if he were flying. And again, if depression or despair has come into his life this has an effect upon that center. A man feels his throat choked and his breath is laden as with a heavy load.

But the heart is not only that. To understand this one should picture a mirror standing before the heart, focused upon the heart, so that every thing and every feeling is reflected in this mirror which is in the physical being of man. Just as man is ignorant of his soul, so he does not know where his heart is nor where the center is where his feelings are reflected. It is a fact known to scientists that when a child is formed it begins from the heart, but a mystic's conception is that the heart, which is the beginning of form, is also the beginning of the spirit which makes man an individual. The depth of that spirit is in reality what we call the heart. Through this we understand that there is such a thing as a heart which is the deepest depth of man's being.

In these days people attribute less importance to sentiment and rely more upon the intellect. The reason for this is that when they meet the two kinds of people, the intellectual and the sentimental, they find greater balance in an intellectual man than in the one with much sentiment. This is no doubt true, but the very reason for the lack of balance is that there is a greater power than the intellect, and this power is sentiment. The earth is fruitful, but not as powerful as the water. The intellect is creative, yet not as powerful as the heart and the sentiment. In reality the intellectual man will also prove unbalanced in the end if he has no sentimental side to his being.

Are there not many people of whom one can say, "I like him, love him, admire him, but he closes his heart?" The one who closes his heart neither loves others completely nor allows others to love him fully. Besides, a man who is only intellectual in time becomes sceptical, doubting, unbelieving, and destructive, since there is no power of the heart to balance it. The Sufi considers the devotion of the heart to be the best thing to cultivate for spiritual realization. Many people may not agree, but it is a fact that the one who closes his heart to his fellow man, closes his heart to God. Jesus Christ did not say, "God is the intellect"; He said, "God is love," and therefore if the peace of God can be found anywhere it is not in any church on earth, nor in heaven above, but in the heart of man. The place where one is most certain to find God is in the loving heart of a kind man.

Many people believe that by the help of reason man will act according to a certain standard of morals, but that does not make people good; and even if they seem good or righteous, they are only made so artificially. The prisoners in gaol can all be righteous, but if natural goodness and righteousness can be found anywhere, it is in the spring of the heart from which life rises, and every drop of this spring is a living virtue. This proves that goodness is not man-made; it is man's very being; and if he lacks goodness it is not through lack of training, although training is often most desirable, but because he has not yet found his true self. Goodness is natural; for a normal person it is necessary to be good. No one needs teaching in order to live a good or a righteous life. If love is the torch on his path, it shows him what fairness means, and the honor of his word, charity of heart, and righteousness. Do we not sometimes see a young man, who with all his boisterous tendencies finds a girl whom he begins to love, and who when he really loves her begins to show a change in his life? He becomes gentle, for he must train himself for her sake; he does without things he was never before willing to give up. And in the same way, where there is love forgiveness is not very difficult. A child comes to its mother, even after having offended a thousand times, and asks her forgiveness. There is no one else to go to, and it does not take a moment for the mother's heart to forgive. Forgiveness was waiting there to manifest itself. One cannot help being kind when there is feeling. Someone whose feeling goes out to another person sees when that person needs his feeling, and he strikes a note of sympathy in everyone he meets, finding the point of contact in every soul, because he has love.

There are people who say, "But is it not unwise to give oneself to everyone in outgoing tenderness, as people in general are not trustworthy?" But if a person is good and kind, this goodness ought to become manifest to everyone, and the doors of the heart should not be closed.

Jesus Christ not only told us to love our friends; he went as far as to say we should love our enemies; and the Sufi treads the same path. He considers his charity of heart toward his fellow men to be love for God, and in showing love to everyone, he feels he is giving his love to God. Here the Sufi and the Yogi differ. The Yogi is not unkind, but he says, "I love you all, but I had better keep away from you, for your souls are always groping in darkness, and my soul is in the light. Your friendship will harm my soul, so I had better keep away and love you from afar." The Sufi says, "It is a trial, but it should be tried. I shall take up my everyday duties as they come along." Although he knows how unimportant the things of the world are, and does not overvalue these things, he attends to his responsibilities toward those who love him, like him, depend upon him, follow him; and he tries to find the best way of coming to terms with all those who dislike and despise him. He lives in the world and yet he is not of the world. In this way the Sufi considers that the main principle in the fulfilment of the purpose of his life is to love man.

Those who love their enemies and yet lack patience are like a burning lantern with little oil. It cannot endure, and in the end the flame fades away. The oil in the path of love is patience, and besides this it is unselfishness and self-sacrifice from beginning to end. And he who says, "Give and take," does not know love; he knows business.

Some say, "I have loved dearly once, but I was disappointed." It is as if a man were to say, "I dig in the earth, but when the mud came I was disappointed." It is true that mud came, but with patience he would have reached the water one day. Only patience can endure. Only endurance makes great; the only way of greatness is endurance. It is endurance which makes things valuable and men great.

Imitation gold can be as beautiful as real gold, the imitation diamond as bright as a real diamond. The difference is that the one fails in the test of endurance, and the other stands up to it. Yet man should not be compared with objects. Man has something divine in him, and he can prove this by his endurance in the path of love.

Whom then should one love, and how should one love? Whatever a person loves, whether duty, human beings, art, friends, an ideal, or his fellow creatures, he has assuredly opened the door through which he must pass in order to reach that love which is God. The beginning of love is an excuse; it leads to that ideal of love which is God alone. Some say that they can love God, but not human beings. But this is like saying to God, "I love Thee, but not Thine image." Can one hate the human creatures in which God's image is to be found and yet claim to love

God? If one is not tolerant, not willing to sacrifice, can one then claim the love of the Lord? The first lesson is the widening of the heart and the awakening of the heart is the inner feeling. The sign of saintliness is not in the power of words, not in the high position, either spiritual or intellectual, not magnetism; the saintly spirit only expresses itself in the love of all creatures; it is the continuous springing of love from that divine fountain in the heart of man. When once that fountain is opened it purifies the heart, it makes the heart transparent to see both the outer and the inner world. The heart becomes the vehicle for the soul to see all that is within and without, and then a man not only communicates with another person, but also with God.

VII

Repose

WHEN THE LIPS ARE CLOSED, then the heart begins to speak; when the heart is silent, then the soul blazes up, raising its flame which illuminates the whole of life. It is this idea which demonstrates to the mystic the great importance of silence which is gained by repose. Most people do not know what repose means, because it is something they feel they need when they are tired, while if they were not tired they would never see the necessity for it.

Repose has many aspects. It is one kind of repose when a person retires from the activity of everyday life and finds himself alone in his room. He breathes a breath of thankfulness as he feels, after all his interesting or tiresome experiences, "At last I am by myself." It is not an ordinary feeling. There is a far deeper feeling behind it; it expresses the certainty that there is nothing to attract his mind and nothing which demands his action. At that moment his soul has a glimpse of relief, the pleasure of which is inexpressible; but the intoxication of life from which every man suffers is such that he cannot fully appreciate that moment of relief, which everyone expects, when it is time to retire after the activities of his daily life, whether he be rich or poor, tired or not.

Does this not teach us that there is a great mystery in repose, a mystery of which people are very often ignorant? Besides, we always find that a thoughtful person has repose by nature, and one who has repose is naturally thoughtful. It is repose which makes one more thoughtful, and it is continual action which takes away thoughtfulness even from a sensible person. People working in the telephone, telegraph, or post offices, upon whose mind there is a continual demand, often in time develop impertinence, insolence, and lack of patience. They do not become less sensible; it only means that lack of repose, which weakens their sense of control, makes them give way to such things. This shows that repose is necessary not only for a person on the spiritual path, but for every soul living on the earth, whatever be his grade of evolution or his standing in life. It is the most important thing to be developed in anyone's nature; not only in a grown-up person, but it is something which should be taught from childhood. Nowadays in education people think so much about the different intellectual attainments the child will need in life, and so little about the repose which is so very necessary for a child.

Sometimes cats and dogs prove more intuitive than mankind. Although man is more capable than the animals he does not give himself time to become more intuitive. It often amused me in New York, where one easily becomes exhausted by the noise of trains and trams and elevators and factories, to see that when a person had a little leisure to sit in the train or subway, he at once began looking at the newspapers. All that action was not enough; is it not in the body, then there must be action in the brain! What is it? It is nervousness, a common disease which today has almost become normal health. If everybody suffers from the same disease then this disease may be called normal. But self-control, self-discipline, only comes from the practice of repose, which is helpful not only on the spiritual path but also in one's practical life, in being helpful and considerate.

The mystic therefore adopts the method of repose, and by this he tries to prepare himself to tread the spiritual path. This path is not an outer path; it is an inner path one has to tread, and therefore the spiritual laws and the journey on the spiritual path are quite contrary to the earthly laws and the journey on the outer path. To explain in simple words what the spiritual path is, I would say that it begins by living in communication with oneself, for it is in the innermost self of man that the life of God is to be found. This does not mean that the voice of the inner self does not come to everyone. It always comes, but not everyone hears it. That is why the Sufi, when he starts his efforts on this path, begins by communicating with his true self within; and when once he has addressed the soul, then from the soul comes a kind of reproduction, like that which the singer can hear on a record which has been made of his own voice.

Having done this, when he has listened to what this process reproduces, he has taken the first step in the direction within; and this process will have awakened a kind of echo in his being. Either peace or happiness, light or form, whatever he has wished to produce, is produced as soon as he begins to communicate with himself. When we compare the man who says, "I cannot help being active, or sad, or worried, as it is the condition of my mind and soul," with the one who communicates with himself, it is not long before the self begins to realize the value of this communication.

This is what the Sufis have taught for thousands of years. The path of the Sufi is not to communicate with fairies nor even with God; it is to communicate with one's deepest, innermost self, as if one were blowing one's inner spark into a divine fire. But the Sufi does not stop there, he goes still further. He then remains in a state of repose, and that repose can be brought about by a certain way of sitting and breathing, and also by a certain attitude of mind. Then he begins to become conscious of some part of his being which is not the physical body, but which is above it. The more he becomes conscious of this, the more he begins to realize the truth of the life hereafter. Then it is no longer a matter of his imagination or of his belief; it is his actual realization of the experience which is independent of physical life, and it is in this state that he is capable of experiencing the phenomena of life. The Sufi therefore does not dabble in different wonder-workings and phenomena. Once he realizes this the whole of life becomes a phenomenon, and every moment, every experience, brings to him a realization of that life which he has found in his meditation.

The being of man is a mechanism of body and mind. When this mechanism is in order there is happiness, fullness of life; and when anything is wrong with the mechanism, the body is ill and peace is gone. This mechanism depends upon winding; it is just like a clock which is wound and it then goes for twenty-four hours. So it is in meditation; when a person sits in a restful attitude and puts his mind in a condition of repose, regulating the action of this mechanism by the process of meditation, it is like the winding of a clock. And its effect continues to be felt because the mechanism was put in order.

Thus the belief of a mystic is not an outward belief in a deity he has not seen; the mystic's worship is not only an outer form—by saying prayers and then his worship is finished. Certainly he makes the best use of the outer things and his pursuit is logical and scientific; he will if possible unite them with the mystical conception; but mysticism includes the scientific explanation as well as the realization of the things taught by religion,

things which would have no meaning to an ordinary person.
When an ordinary person reads about the kingdom of God and
heaven, he reads these names but he does not know where
heaven is; he feels that there is a God but there is no evidence
for it. And therefore a large number of intellectual people who
really are seeking the truth are turning away from the outer
religion, because they cannot find its explanation, and conse-
quently they become materialistic. To the mystic the explanation of the whole of religion is the investigation of the self. The
more one explores oneself, the more one will understand all
religions in the fullest light and all will become clear. Sufism is
only a light thrown upon one's own religion like a light brought
into a room where everything one wants is to be found, and
where the only thing that was needed was light.

Of course the mystic is not always ready to give an answer to
everyone who asks. Can parents always answer their children's
questions? There are some questions which can be answered,
and others which should wait for an answer until those who ask
them are able to understand. I used to be fond of a poem which
I did not understand; I could not find a satisfactory explanation.
After ten years, all of a sudden, in one second, a light was
thrown upon it, and I understood. There was no end to my joy.
Does it not show that everything has its appointed time? When
people become impatient and ask for an answer, something can
be answered, something else cannot be answered; but the answer will come in its own time. One has to wait. Has anyone in
the world been able to explain fully what God is, have even the
scriptures and the prophets succeeded in this? God is an ideal
too high and too great for words to explain. Can anyone explain
such a word as love, can anyone say what truth is?

If truth is to be attained it is only when truth itself has begun
to speak, which happens in revelation. Truth reveals itself,
therefore the Persian word for truth is *khuda*, which means self-
revealing, for this word unites God with truth. So God is truth.

One cannot explain either of these words. The only help the mystic can give is by indicating how to arrive at this revelation. No one can teach or learn this; one has to learn oneself. The teacher is only there to guide one toward this revelation. There is only one teacher: God; and the great masters of the world were the greatest pupils; they each knew how to become a pupil.

How is this all taught or brought to the consciousness of those who tread the path of truth? By *Bayat*, by initiation. It is the trust of someone who guides, given to someone who is treading the path. The one who treads the path must be willing to risk the difficulties of the path; to be sincere, faithful, truthful, undoubting, not pessimistic or sceptical, otherwise with all his efforts he will not reach his aim. He must come whole-heartedly, or else he should not come at all. Half-heartedness is of no value. And what is necessary, too, is some intellectual understanding of the metaphysical aspect of life, which some have, but not all; besides this the qualities of the heart are needed, with the divinity of love as a first principle. Then one needs action, such action as will not hinder on the path of truth, such action as creates greater and greater harmony. And finally one needs repose, which makes it possible to learn by one day of silence what would otherwise take a year of study; if only one knows the real way of silence.

VIII

Action

VERY OFTEN A MAN is apt to think that it is study and meditation and prayer which alone can bring him to the way
leading to the goal; but it must be understood that action also
plays an important part. Few indeed know what effect every
action has upon one's life, what power a right action can give,
and what effect a wrong action can have. Man is only on the
lookout for what others think of his actions, instead of being
concerned with what God thinks of them. If man knew what
effect an action produces upon himself, he would understand
that if a murderer has escaped the hands of the policeman, he
has not escaped from the fault he has committed. For he cannot
escape his self; the greatest judge is sitting in his own heart. He
cannot hide his acts from himself. No doubt it is difficult, almost impossible, for a man to judge the acts of other people,
for he does not know what their conditions are. Man can best
judge himself; however wicked he may be, he will not be really
pleased with his wrong actions, or if he is pleased for a moment,
this pleasure will not last.

But what is right and what is wrong? No one can stamp any
deed as right or wrong. But there is a natural sense in man
which distinguishes between right and wrong, just or unjust, a
sense which is to be found even in a child. One also sees the line
and color in art or decoration; one notices when the tablecloth
is not laid straight on the table, when a line that should be
straight is not straight. Even a child knows when things should
be harmonious in line and color. There is a natural tendency in
the heart of man, the natural instrument which masons use for
building a house.

Different religions have taught different morals which were right for the multitude at that time. No doubt the law of the masses must be respected, but the real conception of right and wrong lies in one's deepest self. The soul is not pleased with that which is not right. The soul's satisfaction lies always in something which gives it complete happiness. The whole method of Sufism is based on the practice not only of thought but of action. All religions have been based not only on truth but on action. Things both material and spiritual have been accomplished by action. To the mystic, therefore, action is most important. During my travels from place to place, when I have come in contact with different people and have had the opportunity of staying with them, I have met some who had perhaps never in their lives read a book on theology or studied mysticism, their whole life having been spent in work, business, and industry; and yet I felt a spiritual advancement made naturally by their right actions in life. They had come to a state of purity which perhaps someone else might find by the way of study or meditation.

One might ask, what is the best way to take in everyday life to lead one to life's ideal? The best way of action is to consider harmony as the first principle to be observed; that in all circumstances and situations and conditions one should try to harmonize with one's fellow-creatures. It is easy to say, but most difficult to live; it is not always easy to harmonize. But if we question ourselves as to why it is so difficult, the answer is that it is not always that other people are difficult and not pliable; it is we ourselves who cannot bend. The palm tree that grows straight up cannot harmonize with other trees whose trunks are not so straight and strong.

There are many good people, but they are not always harmonious. There are many true people, but their truth is not always comforting. They may utter a truth which is like a slap in the face to someone. They are just like the palm tree, straight and righteous, yet at the same time not in harmony. A harmonious person can bend, is pliable; he can meet others. There is no doubt that in order to harmonize one has to make sacrifices, one has to bend to people one does not want to bend to; one has to be more pliable than one is by nature, one has to be more clever than one really is; and all these attempts will not succeed unless one makes a great effort, unless one realizes that harmony is the most essential thing in life.

Why does a mystic attribute such great importance to harmony? Because to a mystic his whole life is one continuous symphony, a playing of music, each soul contributing his particular part to the symphony. A person's success therefore depends upon the idea he has of harmony. Very few people in the world pay attention to harmony; they do not know that without it there is no chance of happiness. It is only the harmonious ones who can make others happy and partake of that happiness themselves, and apart from them it is hard to find happiness in the world. The fighter has no peace; battles will be ever increasing; it is the peacemaker who is blessed. No doubt in order to make peace he will have to fight with himself, and in that way he will be able to make peace with others. Whatever a person's education or position in life, he may possess all he wants, but if that one thing is lacking in his life and heart nothing can bring him peace.

Therefore if a man does not show in his actions some of the characteristics of a human being, characteristics which are not to be found in animals, then he has not awakened to human nature. There are certain actions such as eating, drinking, sitting, and walking, which are not different from those of the animals, yet these very same actions can become specially characteristic of human nature when they have a guiding light behind them. For instance when a man thinks he must not return a push when he is pushed by somebody while walking, and instead says, "I am sorry," he shows a tendency which is different from that of an animal, for animals will fight one another and will lower their horns instead of bowing to one another, while their greeting will be a howl. Man will be different.

The special characteristics of man are consideration, refinement, patience, and thoughtfulness. And when once he has practised these, it leads to another action: to the practice of self-sacrifice which in turn leads to a divine action. When man sacrifices his time and his advantages in life for the sake of another whom he loves, respects, or adores, this sacrifice raises him higher than the ordinary standard instead of human beings; his is then a divine nature, not human any more. Then a human being begins to think as God thinks, and his actions become more and more divine; they become the actions of God. That person is greater than the person who merely believes in God, for his own actions have become the actions of God.

The awakened soul sees all the doings of grown-up people as the doings of the children of one Father. He looks upon them as the Father would look upon all human beings on the earth, without thinking that they are Germans or Englishmen or Frenchmen. They are all equally dear to him. He looks upon all full of forgiveness, not only upon those who deserve it, but also upon the others, for the awakened soul understands not only those who deserve but also those who do not deserve, for he understand the reason behind it all. By seeing good in everybody and everything, he begins to develop that divine light which expands itself, throwing itself upon the greater part of life, making the whole of life a scene of the divine sublimity.

The mystic develops a wider outlook on life, and this wider outlook changes his actions. He develops in himself a point of view which may be called a divine point of view. Then he rises to the state in which he feels that all that is done to him comes from God, and when he himself does right or wrong he feels that he does right or wrong to God. To arrive at such a stage is true religion. There can be no better religion than this, the religion of God on earth. This is the point of view which makes a person as God, divine. He is resigned when badly treated, but for his own shortcomings he will take himself to task, for all his actions are directed toward God.

The conception that the mystic has of the Deity is not only that of a King or a Judge or a Creator; the mystical conception of God is that of the Beloved, the only Beloved there is. To Him all the love of this world is like that of little girls playing with their dolls, loving them. In that way they learn the lessons they have to practice later in life when taking care of the home. The mystic learns the same lessons by proving sincere and devoted to all kinds of creatures, and this he must do in order to awaken himself to the Beloved, the only Beloved there is, to whom all love is due.

THE PATH OF
INITIATION AND
DISCIPLESHIP

I

The Path of Initiation

VERY MUCH HAS BEEN WRITTEN and very much has been said about the path of initiation, and people who have been in contact with various schools of occultism have understood it in different ways, and thus have different ideas as to what initiation means. But in point of fact initiation only means a step forward, a step which should be taken with hope and courage, for without courage and hope it would be most difficult to take any forward step.

If I were asked to explain the meaning of initiation in plain words, I would say that it is like the experience of a person who has never learnt how to swim, and he steps into the river or into the sea for the first time, without knowing whether he will be able to float or whether he will be swept away and drowned. Every person has had an initiation in the worldly sense in some form or other. When a businessman begins an entirely new enterprise, and there is nothing to support him at this moment except the thought, "No matter whether I lose or gain, I will take a step forward, I will go into this enterprise although I do not know what will happen later," he undergoes a worldly initiation. And the first attempt of a man who wants to learn to ride, if he has never been on horseback before nor driven a horse, so that he does not know where the horse will take him— this also is an initiation.

But initiation in the real sense of the word, as it is used on the spiritual path, takes place when a person, in spite of having a religion and belief, an opinion and ideas about spiritual things, feels that he should take a step in a direction which he does not know; when he takes the first step, that is an initiation. Ghazali, a great Sufi writer of Persia, has said that entering the spiritual path is just like shooting an arrow at a point one cannot see, so that one does not know what the arrow is going to hit; one only knows one's own action, and one does not see the point aimed at. This is why the path of initiation is difficult for a worldly man. Human nature is such that a man born into this world, who has become acquainted with the life of names and forms, wants to know everything by name and form; he wants to touch something in order to be sure that it exists. It must make an appeal to his physical senses before he thinks that it exists; without this he does not believe that anything can exist. Therefore it is difficult for him to undergo an initiation on a path which does not touch any of his senses. He does not know where he is going.

Besides, man has been taught from his childhood a certain faith or belief, and he feels himself so bound to that particular faith or religion that he trembles at every step he may have to take in a direction which perhaps for a moment seems different or even opposite to what he has been taught. Therefore to take the first step on the path of initiation is difficult for a thoughtful person. No doubt a person who is driven by curiosity may jump into anything, but it is all the same to him whether he has initiation or not. However, for the one who takes initiation seriously the first step is the most difficult.

Initiations, according to the mystics, are twelve in number, divided into four stages; just like the semitones in the octave, or the twelve bones in the ear. The first three initiations are the first three steps, taken with the help of a guide whom one calls in Sufi terms a Murshid, a teacher. In Vedantic terms he is called Guru. He will be someone who is walking this earth, a human being placed in the same conditions as everyone else, in the midst of active life, and subject to all trials and troubles and difficulties. The help of such a friend is the first and most important step in these first three stages of the path.

In the East one will rarely find people taking the spiritual path without the guidance of a teacher, for there it is an accepted fact that these first three steps at least must be taken with the help of someone living a human life on earth. We can trace in the traditions that all the prophets, masters, saints, and sages, however great, had an initiator. In the life of Jesus Christ one reads that he was baptized by John the Baptist; and in the lives of all the other prophets and seers there was always someone, however humble or modest or human, and very often not at all comparable in greatness to those prophets, who took these first three steps with them. But the mother is really the first initiator of all the prophets and teachers in the world; no prophet or teacher, no saint, however great, was ever born who first walked alone without the help of the mother; she had to show him how to walk.

Then there arises the question of how to find the real guru. Very often people are in doubt, they do not know whether the guru they see is a true or a false guru. Frequently a person comes into contact with a false guru in this world where there is so much falsehood. But at the same time a real seeker, one who is not false to himself, will always meet with the truth, with the real, because it is his own real faith, his own sincerity in earnest seeking that will become his torch. The real teacher is within, that lover of reality is one's own sincere self, and if one is really seeking truth sooner or later one will certainly find a true teacher. And supposing one came into contact with a false teacher, what then? Then the real One will turn the false teacher also into a real teacher, because reality is greater than falsehood.

There is a story told of a dervish, a simple man, who was initiated by a teacher, and after that teacher has passed away this man came into contact with some clairvoyant who asked him if he had guidance on his path. The man replied, "Yes, my master, who passed from this earth. When he was still alive I enjoyed his guidance for some time, so the only thing I would

want now is just your blessing." But the clairvoyant said, "I see
by my clairvoyant power that the teacher who has passed away
was not a true teacher." When the simple man heard this he
would not allow himself to be angry with the other, but he said
gently, "This teacher of mine may be false, but my faith is not
false, and that is sufficient."

As there is water in the depths of the earth so there is truth
at the bottom of all things, false or true. In some places one has
to dig deep, in other places only a short distance, that is the only
difference, but there is no place where there is no water. One
may have to dig very, very deep in order to get it, but in the
depths of the earth there is water, and in the depths of all this
falsehood which is on the surface there is truth. If we are really
seeking for the truth we shall always find it at some time or
other.

The one who wants to protect himself from being misguided
shows a certain tendency, a kind of weakness, which comes
from thinking deep in himself that there is no right guidance. If
he realizes that right guidance is to be found in himself, he will
always be rightly guided; and his power will become so great
that if his guide is going wrong, the power of the pupil will help
him to go right, because the real Teacher is in the heart of man.
The outward teacher is only a sign. A Persian poet has said that
he who is a lost soul, even if he is in the presence of a savior,
will be lost just the same, because his own clouds are surround-
ing him. It is not a question of a guide or teacher; the obscurity
which his own mind creates surrounds him and keeps him
blind. What then can a teacher do?

According to a story about the Prophet Muhammad, there
lived next door to him a man who was very much opposed to
the Prophet and spoke against him; and this man saw that the
people to whom he spoke had belief in the Prophet, while nobody believed in him. Then years passed, and many believed
and many gave their life for the message of the Prophet; and it

so happened that eventually a great many people came from afar, thousands and thousands from different countries, to visit the Prophet. The same man still lived in the neighbourhood, but he had never altered his opinion. And one day someone asked the Prophet, "Why does this man, who has known the day when nobody listened, when nobody followed you, but who now sees that thousands of people who come here are benefited and filled with bliss and joy and blessing, still continue to criticize you and to oppose you?" And the Prophet said, "His heart has become a fountain of obscurity; he produces from his own self the clouds which surround him; he cannot see." And he was sorry for him. The perception of the light shows the thinning of the veil that covers the heart, and the thinner the veil becomes, the greater is the power of the light within.

The next step, the second step in initiation, is to go through the tests that the teacher gives. In this initiation there is a great deal that is amusing, if one thinks about it. It is like looping the loop; sometimes the teacher gives the pupil such tests that he does not know where he is, or whether a thing is true or false. There was a great Sufi teacher in India who had a thousand adherents who were most devoted pupils. One day he said to them, "I have changed my mind." And the words "changed my mind" surprised them greatly; they asked him, "What is the matter, how can it be that you have changed your mind?" He said, "I have the feeling that I must go and bow before the goddess Kali." And these people, among whom were doctors and professors, well qualified people, could not understand this whim, that their great teacher in whom they had such faith wished to go into the temple of Kali and bow before the Goddess of the hideous face, he, a God-realized man in whom they had such confidence! And the thousand disciples left him at once, thinking "What is this? It is against the religion of the formless God, against the teaching of this great Sufi himself, that he wants to worship the goddess Kali!" And there remained only one pupil, a youth who was very devoted to his teacher, and he followed him when he went to the temple of Kali. The teacher was very glad to get rid of these thousand pupils, who were full of knowledge, full of their learning, but who did not really know him; it was just as well that they should leave. And as they were going toward the temple, he spoke three times to this young man, saying "Why do you not go away? Look at these thousand people, who had such faith and such admiration, and now I have said just one word, and they have left me. Why do you not go with them? The majority is right." The pupil, however, would not go, but continued to follow him. And through all this the teacher received great inspiration and a revelation of how strange human nature is, how soon people are attracted and how soon they can fly away. It was such an interesting phenomenon for him to see the play of human nature that his heart was full of feeling, and when they arrived at the temple of Kali he experienced such ecstasy that he fell down and bowed his head low. And the young man who had followed him did the same.

When he got up he asked this young man again, "Why do you not leave me when you have seen a thousand people go away? Why do you follow me?" The young man answered, "There is nothing in what you have done that is against my convictions, because the first lesson you have taught me was that nothing exists save God. If that is true, then that image is not Kali; it too is God. What does it matter whether you bow to the East or to the West or to the earth or to heaven? Since nothing exists except God, there is nobody else except God before whom to bow, even in bowing before Kali. It was the first lesson you taught me." All these learned men were given the same lesson, they were students and very clever, but they could not conceive of that main thought which was the center of all the teaching. It was this same young man who later became the greatest Sufi teacher in India, Khwaja Moin-ud-Din Chishti.

Every year thousands of people of all religions make pilgrimages to his tomb at Ajmer, Hindus, Mohammedans, Jews, and Christians. To the Sufi all religions are one.

There are tests of many kinds that the teacher may give to his pupil to test his faith, his sincerity, his patience. Before a ship puts to sea the captain goes and makes sure that everything is in order for the voyage; and such is the duty of the teacher. Of course it is a very interesting duty. Besides the path of the mystic is a very complex path. What he says may perhaps have two meanings: the outer meaning is one and the inner meaning is another. What he does may also have two meanings, an outer and an inner meaning, and a person who only sees things outwardly cannot perceive the inner meaning. Because he only sees their outer aspect, he cannot understand his own teacher's action, thought, speech, or movement. It is in this way that the pupil is tested.

Thus to the pupil the teacher may often appear to be very unreasonable, very odd, very meaningless, very unkind and cold and unjust. And during these tests, if the faith and the trust of the pupil do not endure he will step back from this second initiation, but if he endures through all this then comes the third step, the third initiation.

The third initiation consists of three stages: receiving the knowledge attentively; meditating upon all one has received patiently; assimilating all the outcome of it intelligently. Thereby the mission of the teacher in this world is completed. Gratitude still remains, but the principal work is finished.

The fourth initiation the seeker gets from his ideal. And who is this ideal, who can give this initiation? No living creature on earth, however great, can prove to be the ideal of anyone else; he may for a certain time, but not forever. The great ones like Buddha, Zoroaster, Christ, and Krishna, who have been the ideal of humanity for thousands of years, when did they become the ideal? During their lifetime? During their lifetime they gave

a sense of being the ideal, they left impressions which afterward
proved them to be the ideal, but during their lifetime they could
not prove it. Why is this? The reason is that even perfect man is
limited in the imperfect garb of humanity. The human limitation covers perfection. However great, however deep, however
spiritual a person is, with all his goodness, with all his inspiration and power, he remains limited. His thought, speech, word,
and action are all limited. A man cannot make himself as his
pupil imagines him. Imagination goes further than the progress
of man; the imagination of every person is his own, and therefore one can only make one's ideal oneself. No one has the
power to make the ideal of another person, and therefore it is
the impression of the great saviors of humanity, it is their goodness, it is whatever little grain of an ideal they have left behind
them that becomes just like a seed, and that seed put into the
soil of the devotee's heart develops into a plant and bears fruit
and flowers as it is reared. So in this fourth initiation there is
this ideal of man's imagination. He may call it Christ or Buddha, he may call it Muhammad or Moses or Zoroaster; it is his
ideal; it is he who has made it; it is his savior, and certainly it
will save him if he considers it to be his savior. But he has to
make it; if he does not make it, the saviour will not save him.
When once he has made his saviour, then he is face to face with
that perfection which his heart has created; then this impression
of Christ or Buddha with which he has impressed himself flowers and grows into a tree, and bears the flowers and fruit which
he has desired. No doubt this initiation is a phenomenon in
itself. Once this initiation is received man begins to radiate, to
radiate his initiator who is within him as his ideal.

Then there is the second stage which is the fifth initiation.
And in the fifth initiation man does not imagine his ideal, but
finds his ideal a living entity within himself, a friend who is
always close to him, within him; he can just bow his head and
see his friend—he is there. To the real devotees of Christ, Christ

is near, as near as they are to themselves to their own self. In times of trouble, in difficulties, he is always there.

The third stage, which is the sixth initiation, is the one where Christ speaks, where Christ acts; the acts of the initiate become the actions of Christ, his speech becomes the speech of Christ. And when one has arrived at that initiation one need not declare before humanity how greatly one loves one's Lord or Savior or Master; the initiate himself becomes a proof, his life, his word, his action, his feeling, his attitude, his outlook.

Life is such that no falsehood, no pretence can endure, nothing false can go far; it will only go a step and then it will tumble down; it is only the real which will go on. And the more real something is, the less it expresses itself. It is lack of reality that makes a person say: he is so and so, he has such great love for God; or he is so spiritual or pious or clairvoyant, or he has such psychic power. When one sees one does not need to say that one sees, everybody will notice that one is not blind.

But how different it is today, when so many people ask, "Are you clairvoyant, can you see?" And if they say they do, what do they see? They have perhaps seen some color or some light here and there, or something peculiar, which means nothing. Perhaps it is their imagination. And then there are others who encourage them and make them still more crazy; and people feed their pride by telling others how much they see. But when one begins to see one cannot speak about it, it is something which cannot be told. How could one? When one sees with the eyes of Christ one can only see, when one hears with the ears of Christ one can only hear; there is nothing to be said.

The further initiation, which is the seventh, is the initiation in God. There is an account in the story of Rabia, a great Sufi. Once in her vision she saw the Prophet, and the Prophet asked her, "Rabia, to whom have you given your devotion?" And Rabia said, "To God." And the Prophet said, "Not to me?" And Rabia said, "Yes, Prophet, you include God, but it is God I gave my devotion to." There comes a stage where a person even rises above the ideal he has made. He rises to that perfect Ideal which is beyond the human personality, which is the perfect Being. In this initiation one rises to the spheres where one sees no other than God.

In the second stage, which is the eighth initiation, one communicates with God, so that God becomes to the initiate a living entity; God is then no longer an ideal or an imagination, no longer one whom he has made; the One whom he once made has now become alive—a living God. Before this there was belief in God, there was worship of Him; perhaps He was made in the imagination; but in this stage God becomes living. And what a phenomenon this is! This stage is a miracle in itself. The God-realized person need not speak of or discuss the name of God; his presence will inspire the sense of God in every being, and charge the atmosphere with it. Everyone that meets him, whether he is spiritual or moral or religious or without religion, will feel God in some form or other.

The prophets and the holy one who have come from time to time to give the world a religion, an ideal, have not brought any new ideas; they have not brought a new belief in God, because belief in God has always existed in some form or other. What they brought was a living God. When there remained no more than God's name in the scripture or in the people's imagination or on the lips of the followers of a certain religion, and when that name began to become a profane name, a vain repetition, then such souls were born on the earth and brought with them a living God. If they gave anything else to humanity, either law, ethics, or morals, these were secondary. The principal thing that they gave to the world was a living God.

The ninth initiation is what is called in Sufi terms *Akhlak-e Allah,* which means the Manner of God. The one who touches that plane or that realization expresses in his manner the manner of God; his outlook on life is God's outlook; his action, his thought, and his word are God's action, thought, and word. Therefore, what the prophets spoke was *Kalam-ullah*, the Word of God, as for instance the Bhaghavat Gita which means the Song Celestial. Why? Because at this stage God himself speaks. These holy ones became that perfect Spirit and were moved by it. They became actors, for their action was no longer their own action; it was the action of God. Their words was no longer a human word; it was the word of God.

Very few arrive at the last three initiations in their lifetime, for after the first nine initiations begins what is called the phase of self-realization. When those who have not arrived at this stage begin to utter affirmations such as "I am God," they utter nothing but vain repetitions, and this obscures the God-ideal. They do not know what they are saying. If people only knew to what an extent they should be authorized before speaking about such things, they would be very careful about what they say.

When after having gone through all the other stages of consciousness one arrives at this stage, one can speak very little; for it is beyond the stage of religion and even beyond the notion of God; it is the stage of self-expression. This stage of self-expression is reached when a person has thoroughly dug his self out, so that nothing of the self is left but only that divine substance; and only then is he authorized to express himself. Thus the tenth initiation is the awakening of the real self, the real ego, and this awakening is brought about by meditation, the meditation which makes one forget one's false or limited self. The more one is able to forget it, the more the real self awakens.

In the next stages one experiences a sensation of splendor, which in Persian is called *Hairat*. It is like when a child is born and begins to see everything new: this old world is seen by the child as a new world. As soon as the point of view is changed by the help of meditation, one sees the whole world, which is before everybody and which everybody is seeing, quite differently. One begins to see reason behind reason, cause behind cause, and one's point of view also changes in regard to religion. It changes because where the average man would want to accuse or punish or blame a person for a certain action, the one who has risen to this stage can neither judge nor blame; he only sees; but he sees the cause behind the cause. Whom then shall he accuse? Whom shall he blame? How can he refrain from forgiving, whatever be the fault, when he sees all that is behind the fault, when he sees the reason behind it, perhaps a more valid reason than even the one who committed the fault can see himself. Therefore naturally the manner of continually sacrificing, the manner of spontaneous love and sympathy, the manner of respect both for the wise and foolish, for the deserving and the undeserving, arises and expresses itself as divine life. It is at this stage that the human soul touches perfection and becomes divine, and that it fulfills its real purpose in life.

II

The Meaning of Initiation

THE MEANING OF THE WORD *initiation* can be understood from its association with *initiative*. It is a fact that every child which is born on earth is born with initiative; but then, as it grows, that spirit more or less dies away, because the knowledge it gathers in its lifetime makes it doubt. This doubt, increasing more and more, very often makes a man lose the power of initiative, and then he does not want to take another step until he is sure whether there is land or water in front of him, and very often water looks like land, and land looks like water. According to the mystics life is an illusion, and thus man bases his reason upon illusion. Nevertheless, the reasoning power which he acquires helps him in his life in the world, although it is very often just this reasoning which holds him back from taking what is called the initiative.

It is through this spirit of initiative that anyone in the world who has accomplished something great has been able to do so. At the beginning of his efforts people call such a person mad or fanatical, or crazy, or devoid of reason, but when they see the result they think that he is most wise. Great prophets, the builders of nations, famous inventors, and great discoverers have all proved this. One may ask then if they do not see what is before them in the same way that a reasoning person does. They do, but with different eyes. Their point of view is different; it does not always agree with the point of view of the average person, and so it is natural that people should call them fanatical, although they see perhaps more than do all those around them. Those who have helped themselves to achieve success after complete failure, or to get over an illness after great suffering, have only succeeded in this by the spirit of initiative.

There are different kinds of initiation that souls experience. One is natural initiation. A kind of natural unfoldment for which the soul cannot give any cause or reason, comes to a soul, although no effort or attempt has been made by that soul to experience it. Sometimes this initiation comes after great illness, pain, or suffering. It comes as an opening up of the horizon, it comes as a flash of light, and in a moment the world seems transformed. It is not that the world has changed; it is that that person has become tuned to a different pitch. He begins to think differently, feel differently, see and act differently; his whole condition begins to change. One might say of him that from that moment he begins to live. It may come as a vision, as a dream, as a phenomenon—in any of these forms; one cannot determine the manner in which it will manifest.

Another initiation known to the mystics is the initiation that one receives from a person living on the earth. Every mystical school has its own initiation. In the Orient, where mystical ideas are prevalent and are regarded as most sacred, any person who wishes to tread the spiritual path considers initiation to be the most important thing. If a soul such as Jesus Christ had to be baptized by John the Baptist, no soul on earth can say, "I have risen above initiation." Is that then impossible? Nothing is impossible. It may be possible for a person to jump into the water with the intention of swimming to the port of New York, but his life will be more secure if he books his passage with the normal shipping lines. And the difference between these two souls is the same, or even greater—between the one who wishes to journey on the spiritual path by taking initiation, and the other who refuses to do so.

Initiation by a spiritual teacher means both a trust given by the teacher to the pupil, and a trust given by the pupil to the teacher. And the progress of the one who is initiated depends upon how much he gives himself to the teacher's guidance. One might give only a finger, another even a part of a finger, while a third would give his whole hand. That makes a great difference, for if a pupil says, "Well, I will give a certain amount of my time and thought to your guidance, will that be enough?" the teacher will say, "Yes, if you think it is enough"; but in reality it is never enough. Then one might wonder if one would not be giving up one's own point of view in order to follow someone else's point of view; but actually if one has a point of view, one never loses it. The point of view which one loses is not one's own. And by looking at a thing from another person's point of view one only enlarges one's own: then one has two points of view instead of one. If the thought of the pupil happens to be different from that of the teacher, by taking the teacher's thought his own is doubled; the pupil keeps his own point of view just the same, only now he has something for his vision from which to make his choice; the horizon of his thought is expanded. But the pupil who closes himself and says, "I will guard my point of view or it will escape me," will never derive any benefit from this attitude.

The mystical path is the most subtle path to tread. The relationship between teacher and pupil is too subtle for words to express. Besides, the language of a mystical teacher is always elusive; you cannot, so to speak, pin him down as to his words; you cannot ask him to say clearly that something is so and so, or such and such. And if a mystic does so he is not a mystic, for a mystic cannot do this. The mystic may seem to be standing on the earth, but he is flying in the air. The air cannot be made into a rock, nor can the mystic be made into a gross entity. His yes does not mean the same as the yes of another, nor does his no mean the same as the no of others. The language of the mystic is not the language of words; it is the language of meaning. It is the greatest distress for a mystic to have to use the words of everyday language, which are not his words. He cannot express himself in these words. And we find the same in the action of the mystic. His outward actions will not express to everybody the meaning which is behind them, and that meaning may be much more important inwardly than the action is outwardly.

The teacher therefore tests his pupil continually. He tells him and he does not tell him, for everything must come in its right time. Divine knowledge has never been taught in words, nor will it ever be so taught. The work of a mystical teacher is not to teach but to tune, to tune the pupil so that he may become the instrument of God. For the mystical teacher is not the player of the instrument; he is the tuner. When he has tuned it, he gives it into the hands of the player whose instrument it is to play. The duty of the mystical teacher is his service as a tuner.

Dispute with a spiritual teacher is never any good. For the pupil may be speaking one language while the teacher speaks another, and when there is no common language, how can the dispute be profitable? Therefore in the path of mysticism there is no dispute.

Also, there are no fixed rules to follow on this path. For every person there is a special rule. But there is one law which applies to everything in life: sincerity, which is the only thing that is asked by a teacher of a pupil, for truth is not the portion of the insincere.

Several initiations may be given to the pupil whom the teacher has taken in hand, but his progress depends upon the pupil himself. Just as parents are anxious, so the spiritual teacher is naturally anxious to see the advancement of his pupil. There is no reason for the teacher to keep any pupil back from success; for as the happiness of the parents lies in the happiness of the child, so the satisfaction of the teacher lies in the advancement of the pupil.

But then there is another kind of initiation which comes afterward, and this initiation is also an unfoldment of the soul. It comes as an aftereffect of the initiation that one had from the teacher. It comes as a kind of expansion of consciousness, and the greatness of this initiation depends upon the distance and width of the horizon of the consciousness. Many may claim it, but few realize it. Those who realize do not claim. As the more fruitful a tree is the more it bends, so the more divine his spiritual realization is the more humble a person becomes. It is the one who is less fruitful who becomes more pretentious. The really initiated ones hardly ever mention the word initiation; they find no profit in convincing others that they are initiated. They possess their real inner gains so they do not want an outer gain; it is the one who has not got any who wants recognition from outside. And if we ask what profit we derive from initiation, the answer is that religion, mysticism, or philosophy—all that we gain—should help us to achieve one result, and that is to be best fitted for serving our fellow-men.

It may be asked whether it is desirable for every soul to take initiation. The word *initiation* and the associated word *initiative* suggest going forward, so the answer is that progress is life and standing still is death. Whatever be our grade of evolution, it is always advisable to try to go forward, be it in business or in a profession, in society or in political life, in religion or in spiritual advancement. No doubt there is a danger in being too enthusiastic. The nature that is too enthusiastic may, instead of benefiting, perhaps harm itself in whatever line it may have taken up, worldly or spiritual. For everything there is a time, and patience is necessary in all striving. A cook may burn food by applying more heat in order to cook more quickly, and this rule applies to all things. With little children the parents are often anxious and enthusiastic; they think their children should learn and understand every good and interesting thing on earth. Too much enthusiasm is not right. We must give time to all things; the first and most important lesson in life is patience; we must begin all things with patience.

The Sufi Order is mainly an esoteric school. There are three principal esoteric schools known in the East: the Buddhist school, the Vedantic school, and the Sufi school. The two former use asceticism as their principal means of spiritual advancement; the peculiarity of the Sufi school is that it uses humanity as its chief means to the same end. In the realization of truth the Sufi school is no different from the Vedantic or the Buddhist, but the Sufi presents truth in a different manner. It is the same frame in which Jesus Christ has given His teaching.

No doubt the method of helping spiritual development by contemplation and meditation is used in all three schools, the science of breath being the foundation of each; but the Sufi thinks that man was not created as man to live the life of an angel, neither was he created to live the life of an animal. For the life of an angel, angels are created, and for the life of an animal there are animals. The Sufi thinks that the first thing which is necessary for man in life is to prove to his own conscience to what extent he can be human. It is not only a spiritual development, it is the culture of humanity: in what relation man stands to his neighbor or friend, to those who depend upon him and those who look up to him, to strangers unknown to him; how he stands with those younger than himself and with older people, with those who like him and others who dislike him and criticize him; how he should feel and think and act through life, and yet keep on progressing toward the goal which is the goal for every soul in the world. It is not necessary for the Sufi to seek the wilderness for his meditation, since he can perform part of his work in the midst of worldly life. The Sufi need not prove himself a Sufi by extraordinary power, by wonder-working or by an exceptional spiritual manifestation or claim. A Sufi can prove to his own conscience that he is a Sufi by watching his own life amidst the strife of this world.

There are some who are content with a belief taught at home or in church. They are contented, and they may just as well rest in that stage of realization where they are contented until another impulse is born in their hearts to rise higher. The Sufi does not force his belief or his thoughts upon such souls. In the East there is a saying that it is a great sin to awaken anyone who is fast asleep. This saying can be symbolically understood: that there are many in this world who work and do things and are yet asleep; they seem awake externally, but inwardly they are asleep. The Sufi considers it a crime to awaken them, for some sleep is good for their health. The work of the Sufi is to give a helping hand to those who have had sufficient sleep and who now begin to stir in their sleep, to turn over. And it is that kind of help which is the real initiation.

No doubt there are things which pass the ordinary comprehension of man. There are things one can teach only by speaking or by acting, but there is a way of teaching which is called *Tawajoh* and this way of teaching is without words. It is not external teaching; it is teaching in silence. For instance, how can man explain the spirit of sincerity, or the spirit of gratefulness? How can man explain the ultimate truth, the idea of God? Whenever it has been attempted it has failed; it has made some confused, and it has made others give up their belief. It is not that the one who tried to explain did not understand, but that words are inadequate to explain the idea of God.

In the East there are great sages and saints who sit quite still, with lips closed, for years. They are called *Muni*, which means "he who takes the vow of silence." The man of today may think, "What a life, to be silent and do nothing!" But he does not know that some by their silence can do more than others can accomplish by talking for ten years. A person may argue for months about a problem and not be able to explain it, while another, with inner radiance, may be able to answer the same thing in one moment. But the answer that comes without words explains still more. That is initiation.

However, no one can give spiritual knowledge to another, for this is something which is within every heart. What the teacher can do is to kindle the light which is hidden in the heart of the disciple. If the light is not there, it is not the fault of the teacher.

There is a verse by Hafiz in which he says, "However great be the teacher, he is helpless with the one whose heart is closed." Therefore initiation means initiation on the part of the disciple and on the part of the teacher, a step forward on the part of both. On the part of the teacher, a step forward with the disciple in order that the pupil may be trusted and raised from his present condition. A step forward for the pupil, because he opens his heart; he has no barrier any more, nothing to hinder the teaching in whatever form it comes, in silence or in words, or in the observation of some deed or action on the part of the teacher.

In ancient times the disciples of the great teachers learned by a quite different method, not an academic method or way of study. The way was that with open heart, with perfect confidence and trust, they watched every attitude of the teacher both towards friends and towards people who looked at him with contempt; they watched their teacher in times of trouble and pain, how he endured it all; they saw how patient and wise he had been in discussing with those who did not understand, answering everyone gently in his own language; he showed the mother-spirit, the father-spirit, the brother-spirit, the child-spirit, the friend-spirit, forgiving kindness, an ever tolerant nature, respect for the aged, compassion for all, the thorough understanding of human nature. This also the disciples learnt: that no discussion or books on metaphysics can ever teach all the thoughts and philosophy that arise in the heart of man. A person may either study for a thousand years, or he may get to the source and see if he can touch the root of all wisdom and all knowledge. In the center of the emblem of the Sufis there is a heart; it is the sign that from the heart a stream rises, the stream of divine knowledge.

On the path of initiation two things are necessary: contemplation, and the living of a life such as a Sufi ought to live; and they depend upon each other. Contemplation helps one to live the life of a Sufi, and the life of a Sufi helps contemplation. In the West, where life is so busy and where there is no end to one's responsibilities, one wonders if to undertake contemplation, even for only ten minutes in the evening, is not too much when one is tired. But for that very reason contemplation is required more in the West than in the East where everything, even the surroundings, is helpful to contemplation. Besides, a beginning must be made on the path. If contemplation does not develop in such a form that everything one does in life becomes a contemplation, then the contemplation does not do a person any good. It would be like going to church once a week and forgetting all about religion on the other days. To a man who gives ten or twenty minutes every evening to contemplation and forgets it all the rest of the day, contemplation will not do any good. We take our food at certain times every day; yet all the time, even when we are sleeping, the food nourishes our body. It is not the Sufi's idea to retire in seclusion or to sit silent all day. His idea is that by contemplation he becomes so inspired that in study, in every aspiration, in every aspect of life, progress is made. In this way he proves his contemplation to be a force helping him to withstand all the difficulties that come to him.

The life that the Sufi ought to live may be explained in a few words. There are many things in the life of a Sufi, but the greatest is to have a tendency to friendship; this is expressed in the form of tolerance and forgiveness, in the form of service and trust. In whatever form he may express it this is the central theme: the constant desire to prove one's love for humanity, to be the friend of all.

III

What Is Needed on the Path

INITIATION NEEDS COURAGE and the tendency to advance spiritually, although it may not seem to be the way of life for everyone. Therefore the first duty of a mureed is not to be shaken in his faith by any opposing influence or by anything said against the path he has taken. He should not allow himself to be discouraged by anybody. The mureed must be so firm in his path that if the whole world says it is a wrong path, he will say it is the right path. And if anybody says that it will take a thousand years or perhaps more, the mureed must be able to say that even if it should take a thousand years, he will have the

patience to go through with it. As it is said in Persian, it is the
work of the *Baz,* the wayfarer of the heavens.

In this mystical path courage, steadfastness, and patience are
what is most necessary, but also trust in the teacher at whose
hand initiation is taken, and the understanding of the idea of
discipline. In the East, where for thousands of years the path of
discipleship has been understood, these things are regarded as
most important and acceptable from the hand of the teacher.
How few in the world know trust! What is necessary is not
trusting another, even the teacher, but oneself, and one is not
capable of trusting oneself fully when one has not experienced
in life how to trust another. Some will ask, "But if we trusted
and our trust was in vain, should we not be disappointed?" The
answer is that we must trust for the sake of the trust, and not
for the sake of a return and to see what fruit it brings. The
utmost trust is the greatest power in the world. Lack of trust is
weakness. Even if we have lost something by trusting, our power
will be greater than if we had gained something without developing trust.

Patience is very necessary on the path. After my initiation
into the Order of the Sufis I was for six months continually in
the presence of my murshid before he said a word on the subject
of Sufism; and as soon as I took out my notebook he went on
to another subject; it was finished! One sentence after six
months! A person would think that it is a long time, six months
sitting before one's teacher without being taught anything; but
it is not words, it is something else. If words were sufficient,
there are libraries full of occult and mystical books. It is life
itself, it is living that is important. The one who lives the life of
initiation not only lives himself, but also makes others who
come in contact with him alive. Therefore one is initiated into
the Sufi Order not especially for study, but to understand and
follow what real discipleship means.

With regard to the subject of discipline, anybody without a

sense of discipline is without the power of self-control. It is discipline which teaches the ideal, and the ideal is self-discipline. It is the disciplined soldier who can become a good captain. In ancient times the kings used to send the princes out as soldiers, to learn what discipline means. The path of initiation is the training of the ego, and it is self-discipline which is learned on the path of discipleship.

One may ask what one should think of the path of initiation: what must be our goal, what must we expect from it? Should we expect to be good, or healthy, or magnetic, or powerful, or developed psychically, or clairvoyant? None of these does one need to be, although in time one will cultivate them all naturally, but one should not strive for these things.

Suppose a person develops power, and he does not know how to use it, the outcome will be disastrous. Suppose he develops magnetism, and by his power he attracts all, both good and bad; then it will be difficult to get rid of what he has attracted by his power. Or perhaps a person is very good, so good that everyone seems bad to him; he is too good to live in the world, and in that way he will become a burden to himself. These things are not to be sought for through initiation. The aim is to find God within ourselves, to dive deep into ourselves, so that we may touch the unity of the whole Being. It is toward this end that we are working by the power of initiation, in order that we may get all the inspiration and blessing in our life from within.

For this two things are necessary: one is to do the exercises that are given regularly and to do them with heart and soul; the second is to undertake the studies that are given, not considering them to be only for superficial reading, but for every word to be pondered upon. The more one thinks about it, the more it will have the effect of opening the heart. Reading is one thing, contemplating is another. The lessons must be meditated upon; one should not take even the simplest word or sentence for granted. Think of the Hindus, Chinese, Parsis, who for thousands of years have always meditated upon the readings which they held sacred and yet never tired of them.

Initiation is a sacred trust, a trust given by the murshid to his mureed and a trust given by the mureed to the murshid. There should no longer be a wall from the moment of this initiation; for if there is a wall, then the initiation is not an initiation any more. And when the wall between the mureed and the murshid has been removed, then the next step will be for the wall to be removed that stands between God and the worshipper. Besides the Sufi Order is an order of mysticism, and there are certain thoughts and considerations which should be observed. One of these is that when once a secret has been entrusted to one, it must be kept as one's most sacred trust. One must also accept all the teaching that may be given to one; whether it is bitter medicine or sweet, the patient takes it. There is a time for everything, and so illumination has its time. But progress, the real progress, depends upon the patience of the pupil, together with his eagerness to go forward.

The path of initiation is also a path of tests: tests from the initiator, tests from God, tests from the self, and tests from the world; and to go through these tests is the sign of real progress in the mureed, while the one who does not undertake these tests will be wasting his time.

The Order, and this is apparent from the word *order* itself, means that there is a certain formal hierarchy of the initiators and of the Pir-o-Murshid, and that they should be regarded and respected as those who have gone further in that chosen direction. This law is in no way different from the law of nature and of life: when a child who has been disrespectful to its parents itself becomes a parent, it will find the same attitude in its own children. A soldier who does not observe discipline under his captain or colonel will experience the same from his subordinates when later he holds that position. But the question is whether he will ever arrive at that rank, not having considered and observed that which should have been observed; for those who have advanced in any line, whether in music, in poetry, in thought, or in philosophy, have always done so in a humble way, at every step greeting those who have gone further.

Then there are three stages for the pupil, the mureed, who treads the spiritual path. The first stage is receptivity, taking all that is given without saying, "This teaching I will accept and that I will not accept." The next stage is assimilating the teachings. And the third stage is fixing them in the mind and letting the mind see the reason of things; but this comes after assimilation. Thus the one who considers these three stages and goes through them carefully, securely—the stage of receptivity, the stage of assimilation, and the stage of consideration—will be the successful mureed on the path.

Although the outer form might appear to be a hierarchy, yet the Sufi message leads to true democracy, for it holds the promise of that goal which is the yearning of every soul. This itself is the principal thing in democracy, because it is this which makes democracy; and the reason, according to the Sufi belief, is that the divine spark is in every soul. It is with trust and confidence in God, in the murshid, and in that divine spark which is in one's own heart that one is assured of success in life if one will only step forward.

IV

The Different Steps on the Path

THE WORD *initiation* is interpreted by different people in different ways. By some it is considered to be a kind of attachment to a certain secret order, but what I mean by initiation is taking a step forward on a path unknown to oneself.

Initiations are of three different kinds. One initiation comes from within oneself, and this initiation is a person's intention to proceed on a path which is not generally taken by his fellow creatures. If this does not come from within he will always be afraid to take a step further on a path which others around him do not take, for the conception of the generality is not that of an individual. The nature of most people is like that of sheep; wherever sheep are taken, there all the other sheep will follow. One should realize that although it is the nature of sheep to move in a flock this is not the real nature of man. He will always deny that he has this tendency and he will disapprove of it, and yet he will do the very thing without knowing that he does it. If you want to see it, just stand in the street and look up with surprise, acting as if you were absorbed in what you see, and soon twenty persons will be standing by your side, not only foolish people but wise ones too! Therefore he who is initiated, who walks on the path of initiation, is someone who has risen above the crowd, and goes his individual way forward, independent of those who are around him.

When a man begins to feel that there is something behind the veil, when he begins to feel that there is something which he can attain by effort, then he takes the first step on the path which as yet he does not know. One should not be surprised if one notices this initiation in a five-year-old child, neither need one be surprised if one does not see any sign of it in a man of sixty years; he has had no tendency towards it and all his life he has not thought about it. But the one who has received this initiation will go on; even in childhood he will show the tendency to take a step forward on a path which others do not take.

One will find this initiation in all the different aspects of life. A child taking a slate and pencil and drawing a picture, while not being an artist yet has a tendency to draw something, perhaps an idea which is not a child's idea but is very wonderful. One will find a child humming or singing a piece of music which a composer will be surprised to hear. He is doing something which is not ordinary, something which comes spontaneously from his soul and which shows his initiation in that path. One will also hear a child speak on certain subjects, and express ideas which are quite different from what one would expect from a child, ideas which are perhaps even beyond the comprehension of a grown man. Yet the child speaks about it; it is his initiation. I have known a child to ask me, "Why must one kneel down, why must one prostrate oneself when they say that God is above?" and another to say, "Why must there be one direction in which a person should look in order to worship, why should not all directions be equally good for worship?"

Many grown-up people have the fixed idea that they must perform their worship in a certain direction and not in any other, and never once in their lives have they asked themselves why. One will find grown-up people who have perhaps worshipped kneeling down all their life, and have never asked themselves why they should kneel down on the earth when they are supposed to worship God in the heavens. Therefore to believe, to worship, to be pious, to be good is quite different from the idea of being initiated. Initiation means emerging from the ordinary, it is rising above the conditions which are common; and this shows the maturity of the soul.

The second stage is the materialization of this initiation; and this materialization is possible with someone living on the earth. For the condition of being initiated completely is to become initiated on this plane of earth, on the physical plane where one is living and moving and through which one is experiencing life.

People make a great many mysteries out of the name initiation, but the simple explanation of initiation is trust on the part of the pupil and confidence on the part of the initiator. I heard from my murshid, from my initiator, something which I shall never forget, "This friendship, this relationship which is brought about by initiation between two persons is something which cannot be broken, it is something which cannot be separated, it is something which cannot be compared with anything else in the world; it belongs to eternity."

When this initiation takes place it then becomes the responsibility of the initiator to think of the welfare and well-being of his pupil; and it becomes the responsibility of the initiated to be faithful and true and steady and unshaken through all tests and trials. There are some who will go to one person and be initiated, and then afterwards they go to another to be initiated, and then to a third. They might go to a hundred persons, but they will become a hundred times less instead of a hundred times more blessed. For the object of friendship is not the making of many friends, the object is to keep friendship steady, unchanged, whole. And of all kinds of friendship, the friendship that is established by initiation is the most sacred, a friendship which must be considered beyond all other relationships in the world.

There is a story of a peasant in India, a young peasant who used to take a great interest in spiritual things. And someone with a great name happened to come to his town, about whom it was said, as it was always said among simple peasants, that he was so great that by coming into his presence one would be sure to enter the heavens. The whole town went to see him and to get from him that guarantee of entering the heavens, except that peasant who had once been initiated. The great man having heard about his refusal went to his house and asked him, "How is it that you who take such interest in holy subjects did not come, while everyone else came to see me?" He said, "There was no ill-feeling on my part, there was only one simple reason. My teacher who initiated me has passed from this earth, and since he was a man with limitations I do not know whether he has gone to heaven or to the other place. And if through the blessing of your presence I were sent to heaven, I might be most unhappy there; heaven would become another place for me if my teacher were not there."

It is this oneness, this connection, it is this relationship between the initiator and the initiated which gives them the necessary strength, power, and wisdom to journey on this path. For it is the devotion of the initiated which supplies all that is lacking in the initiator, and it is the trust of the initiator which supplies all that is lacking in the initiated.

There is no ceremony that a Sufi considers really necessary, but Sufis never regard ceremonies or dogmas as undesirable, so they are not prejudiced against ceremonies. They have even adopted ceremonies for themselves at different times.

Sufis have various paths of attainment, for instance the paths of Salik and Rind; and among those who tread the path of Salik, of righteousness, there are many whose method of spiritual attainment is devotion. Devotion requires an ideal; and the ideal of the Sufis is the God-ideal. They attain to this ideal by a gradual process. They first take Bayat, initiation, from the hand of one whose presence gives them confidence that he will be a worthy counsellor in life and a guide on the path as yet untrodden, and who at the same time shows them in life the image of the Rasul personality, the personality of the ideal man. He is called Pir-o-Murshid.

There are several steps on the path. This is a vast subject, but condensing it I would say that there are five principal steps. The first is responsiveness to beauty of all kinds, in music, in poetry, in colour or line. The second is one's exaltation by beauty, the feeling of ecstasy. The third step is tolerance and forgiveness, when these come naturally without striving for them. The fourth is that one accepts as if they were a pleasure things one dislikes and cannot stand: in the place of a bowl of wine, the bowl of poison. And the fifth step is taken when one feels the rein of one's mind in one's hand; for then one begins to feel tranquillity and peace at will. This is just like riding on a very vigorous and lively horse, yet holding the reins firmly and making it walk at the speed one desires. When this step is taken the mureed becomes a master.

The time of initiation is meant to be a time for clearing away all the sins of the past. The cleansing of sins is like a bathe in the Ganges. It is the bath of the spirit in the light of knowledge. From this day the page is turned. The mureed makes his vow to the murshid that he will treasure the teachings of the masters in the past and keep them secret, that he will make good use of the teachings and of the powers gained by them, and that he will try to crush his Nafs, his ego. He vows that he will respect all the masters of humanity as the one embodiment of the ideal man, and will consider himself the brother not only of all the Sufis in the Order to which he belongs, but also outside that order of all those who are Sufis in spirit although they may call themselves differently, and of all mankind, without distinction of caste, creed, race, nation, or religion. Sufis engage in *Halka*, a circle of Sufis sitting and practicing *Zikr* and *Fikr* so that the power of the one helps the other. Furthermore they practice *Tawajoh*, a method of receiving knowledge and power from the teacher in silence. This way is considered by Sufis to be the most essential and desirable.

Sometimes a receptive mureed attains in a moment greater perfection than he might attain in many years by study or practice, because it is not only his own knowledge and power that the murshid imparts, but sometimes it is the knowledge and power of Rasul; and sometimes even of God. It all depends upon the time and upon how the expressive and receptive souls are focused.

The task of the Sufi teacher is not to force a belief on a mureed, but to train him so that he may become illuminated enough to receive revelations himself.

V

Inner Study

WHY DO SUFIS STUDY esoteric subjects? Is it for the acquisition of spiritual powers or inspiration, to bring about phenomena, or out of curiosity? If this were so it would be wrong. Is it in order to accomplish something material or for worldly success? That is not desirable. Self-realization, to know what we are, should be the Sufi's aim.

Some people who admire piety and goodness want everyone to be an angel, and discovering that this is impossible they are full of criticism. Man has in him both a devil and an angel; he is at once human and animal. It is the devil in man that drives him to do harm without a motive, by instinct, and the first step should be to abandon this attitude. Although nowadays hardly anyone believes that his particular demon can be a manifestation of the devil, who can say that he is free from such an evil spirit? We can be under the power of a spell, but we must overcome such a power; we must liberate ourselves from evil. Everyone can fight.

We must discover at which times we have manifested our

devil or our animal spirit. We want a human spirit, and self-realization is the search for this human spirit; everything must become human in us. But how should we accomplish this? Read the Bible and other holy scriptures? All these books tell us what we should do, but we must also find the store of goodness that is within us, in our heart. As we cultivate our heart it rises. By asceticism one can develop one's soul and reach ecstasy, but what is the use of samadhi if we are not first human? If we want to live in this world we must be human. The ascetic should live in the forest.

How should we cultivate the heart, the feeling? There is no doubt that harmlessness, devotion, and kindness are necessary; but there is something besides these. It is the awakening of certain centres which make one sensitive, not only externally but also mentally.

There are two kinds of people: one will be struck by the beauty of music or other manifestations of beauty; another is as dull as a stone to all this. Why? Because something in his heart and mind is not awakened. We have five senses, but we also have inner senses, and these can enjoy life much more keenly. Some people will say that they need no inner senses, that the outer senses satisfy them completely. They would speak differently if, for instance, they lost their eyesight or another of their five senses. In order to be complete a human being must also develop his inner senses; but first of all he should develop his inner feeling.

Intellectual study may last the whole of one's life; there is no end to it, and this is why the teacher does not encourage speculation. A doctrine means a separation from other doctrines. The Sufi belongs to every religion, and thus he has no special beliefs and speculations. There can for instance be one Sufi who believes in reincarnation, and another who realizes heaven and hell. The work of the Sufi is personal development.

It is what one practices that is important rather than what the teacher says, though the teacher can give protection.

Initiation contains several degrees. It is a trust given to one by the teacher, but the real initiation is the work of God. No teacher can or will judge. The real pupil is he whom the teacher knows he can trust, though all are welcome to him. Spiritually he is both father and mother to the pupil. The life of the teacher is often a sacrifice; he is often persecuted and suffers much, but what little help he can give, he will give.

No special qualification is needed in order to become a pupil. The teacher gives; the pupil can take it or leave it. The teaching is like a precious jewel hidden in a stone; it is for the pupil to break the stone and find the jewel. In the East this inner teaching is part of religion, whereas in the West it is often looked upon merely as a form of education. It ought to be a sacred education. In the East the murshid gives the lesson and the pupil practices it for a month or a year; he cannot have a different practice every week. My grandfather practiced one meditation for forty years, then a miracle happened to him. One should not be ambitious to do other exercises before having had a result from the first one.

There are different degrees, but they are not to be discussed on this path. Because, after all, different stages are the conceptions, the speculations of some wise people. It is just the same as with music: there are seven notes of music, because the musician has accepted that there are seven, but a scale can be made to contain more notes or less notes if the musician wishes to make it so. We distinguish stages, although in reality it is impossible to do so. It is a spontaneous development on the spiritual path which may be called treading the path of initiation.

How can one explain spiritual progress? What is it? What is it like? Spiritual progress is the changing of the point of view. There is only one way to recognize this progress, and that is to see the progress in one's own outlook on life, to ask oneself the

question, "How do I look at life?" This one can do by not judging others, but by being only concerned with one's own outlook; as long as a person is concerned with the faults of others,
as long as he criticizes others, he is not yet ready to make his
sight clear enough to see if his outlook on life is right.

What in reality are the different initiations? Is one better
than the other, or higher than the other? In what way are they
to be distinguished? By knowing some more mysteries, or by
knowing some secrets, or by studying something very wonderful, or by communicating with something unseen? Nothing
whatever of this kind, not one of these things, can assure one of
a higher initiation, of greater progress in the spiritual life. In the
first place we need not strive for mystery, for life itself is a mystery. All that seems simple to us, all that presents no mystery,
becomes mysterious as soon as the outlook on life is changed.
Secrecy is to be found in simplicity; it is the simple life which is
full of secrets. A person may study a whole library, may write
fifty books and may read a thousand, yet all this leads him no-
where. If any study is required we need not go anywhere else;
our life itself is study, if we will only study it. For one who
studies, life offers every opportunity; from morning to evening,
every moment of the day, in the home, outside, at work, in
leisure, in all things there is something to study. No book can
give the joy and the pleasure that human nature itself can give.

The wise, the foolish, the good, the weak, whom we meet
every day with their tendencies and their attitude, are all the
greatest material for study. Besides, there is so much to study in
success and failure, in sorrows and pleasures, and in all things
in life whether unfavorable or favorable. All that we do right, all
that we do wrong, everything is a lesson, everything is a study if
we take it as such. But the important thing is this, that the one
who is life's student, the one who is really initiated, studies himself before studying others. Does an initiator teach the truth?
No man has the power to teach another the truth; man must

discover it himself. What the initiator can do from his side is to say, "This is the path, do not go astray." The initiator will put his pupil on that path where the further he goes the more he will receive at every step; it is like a hand raising him upward. But the first step is the most difficult, and that step is taken by the help of an initiator on the earth.

What is it that the initiator teaches the initiated one? He tells the initiated one the truth of his own being. He does not tell him something new or something different. He tells him something which his soul already knows but which his mind has forgotten. There is a fable which illustrates this. A lion walking through the desert found a little lion cub playing with some sheep. It happened that the little lion had been reared with the sheep, and so it had never had a chance or an occasion to realize what it was. The lion was greatly surprised to see a lion cub running away and being just as afraid of a lion as sheep are. The lion jumped in among the flock of sheep and said, "Halt, halt!" But the sheep ran away and the little lion ran too. The lion only pursued the lion cub, not the sheep, and when it caught up with it the lion said, "I wish to speak to you." The cub said, "I tremble, I am afraid, I cannot stand before you." The lion said, "Why are you running about with the sheep? You yourself are a little lion!" "No," said the little one. "I am a sheep; let me go, let me go with the sheep." "Come along," said the lion, "come with me and I will show you what you are before I let you go." Trembling and yet helpless, the cub followed the lion to a pool of water. Pointing at their reflections in the pool the lion said, "Look at me and look at yourself. Do we not resemble each other closely? You are not like the sheep, you are like me!"

This lion is symbolical of the souls who become God-conscious, the souls who have realized the truth. And when they see the same divine spirit in another soul, their first thought is to take that soul by the hand and to show it that in it also there is the same divine spark which they possess. Therefore although outwardly it is an aristocratic picture, inwardly it is leading to democracy. The command of the lion to that lion cub is apparently aristocratic, but what is the intention of the lion? It is democracy, it wants to make the little lion conscious of the same grandeur that the lion has. And that is the path of spirituality. Its outward appearance may not seem so, but its inner intention and its culmination are democracy.

The initiations beyond those I have spoken of are greater still. Some people, although not all, will tell you of their experiences, and how at different times in their life a sudden change of outlook came to them. It is not our usual experience to wake up suddenly one day from sleep and find that our point of view has changed; but it is no exaggeration to say that it takes but one moment to change one's outlook on life entirely. This is what an initiation is, an initiation which is above the initiations of the earth as we know them. One thing leads to another, and so we go on in life from one initiation to the next; and each step on the ladder that seems to be standing before us, for us to climb, becomes an initiation. And each step on that ladder changes our point of view if only we hold on to the ladder and do not drop down; for there is always the possibility of going either forward or backward. Nevertheless, the one anxious to go forward will never go backward. Even if the whole world pulled him back by a chain attached to his feet, he would still go forward, because his desire to go forward is more powerful than all the forces of the world.

VI

Three Aspects of Initiation

A S BIRDS GATHER IN FLOCKS and animals in herds, so there are human beings who move in groups in this or that direction drawn by the power of others; and yet if one asked a person if this is the case with him too, he would say, "No; not with me, but with all others." It is difficult for anyone to realize to what extent he can unconsciously move with the crowd to the right or the left. And when a person takes a step in a different direction, dissatisfied with being held and swayed by the crowd, by his friends and relations, by those who surround him, then he shows initiative. So the real meaning of the word *initiation*, which is related to *initiative*, is that a man takes his own direction instead of that in which the crowd is pulling him. And when this happens the religious people will say that he has become a heathen, his friends will say that he has become foolish, and his relations will say that he has gone crazy.

Initiation has three different aspects: one is natural initiation, another is advanced initiation, and the third is higher initiation.

The natural initiation may come to a person at any time of his life. It does not come to everyone, but only to some. And for this initiation one need not go to a teacher; it comes when it is time for it to come. It comes in the form of a sudden change of outlook on life; a person feels that he has suddenly awakened to quite another world; although he remains in the same world it has become totally different to him. Things which seemed important become less important; colors pale and the brightness of things disappears. Things show themselves to have different values. The value of everything changes the moment the outlook is changed. It is a change like looking through a telescope; through a telescope one sees things quite differently.

A person may be young and have that experience; it may come at any time in one's life. To some it comes gradually, but then it is a long process, while to others something suddenly happens in their lives and in the twinkling of an eye the world has become different; everything suddenly has a different value. This is natural initiation.

How is this initiation brought about? What is its metaphysical process? The soul is veiled by covers, one cover over the other, and the rending of these covers allows the soul to emerge or to rise higher. Naturally with the next step the horizon of its outlook becomes wider, and the soul reaches further while life becomes more clear. A person may not be conscious of such a change; he may ignore it or not know about it, yet it is there, even though among a hundred people perhaps only one is really conscious of it.

At every step forward that the soul takes on the path it naturally comes closer to God, and coming closer to God means inheriting or drawing toward oneself the qualities of God. In other words the soul sees more, hears more, comprehends more, and enjoys more, because it lives a greater, a higher life.

The teachers and prophets who had to give a message to humanity, who had to render a service to humanity, had such initiations even in their childhood. There is a symbolical story that the heart of the Prophet Muhammad was opened and some substance was taken out of it. People take this literally; but the real meaning is that a cover was torn away, and the soul was allowed to reach upward and go further on the path. There may be many such initiations, perhaps one or two or six or seven according to the state of evolution of the initiate.

Life as we live it today is very difficult for a person whose outlook is thus suddenly changed, for the world lives nowadays at a certain pitch and it cannot tolerate someone whose pitch is below or above the ordinary pitch of life. People dislike such a one, they make difficulties for him, they disapprove of him and of his ideas; and if he does not have any friend or guide on the path, then he may linger on in the same plane of thought till nature helps him, for everything else pulls him backward.

Some people think that saints, masters, or sages have no need for initiation, but they forget that no soul can go further on the path without initiation.

What is the result of this natural initiation? Bewilderment, extreme bewilderment. But this bewilderment is not the same as confusion; there is a vast difference between the two. In confusion there is an element of doubt, but when a person is bewildered he says, "How wonderful, how marvellous; words cannot explain it; it is a miracle!" It may appear quite simple to someone else, but to an advanced person it is a miracle. And there may be others who say, "How foolish, I do not see anything in what you have seen!" But what one has perceived is so marvellous that it cannot be explained.

Such is life; it is a difference of outlook. One person sees a wonder, a splendor, and another says, "What of it? It is quite simple; it is nothing." And the one who says this thinks that he is superior because to his mind it is simple, while the one who wonders has the outlook of a child, for a child wonders at everything. No doubt it is childlike, but it is the child's soul that sees; it sees more than the soul of a grown-up which has become covered by a thousand veils. In infancy the child can see the angelic world, it can talk with unseen entities, it can see wonderful things belonging to the different planes. It is easy to say of something that it is childlike, innocent, or ignorant; yet it is the most wonderful thing to be childlike and to have the innocence of an infant. There is nothing better to wish for, as in this all happiness and beauty are to be found.

This bewilderment produces a kind of pessimism in a per-

son, but a pessimism which cannot be compared with what we
ordinarily call pessimism. For we regard pessimism as a kind of
wretchedness, but this is something different. A hint of this is
to be found in Omar Khayyám's verse, "O, my Beloved, fill the
cup that clears today of past regret and future fears; tomorrow,
why, tomorrow I may be myself with yesterday's sev'n thousand
years!" This pessimism comes as an upliftment, it makes a person see life from a different angle. The very life which seemed
before to be towering over his head suddenly appears to be beneath his feet.

What is it then? Besides calling it pessimism one could also
call it indifference, or independence, and yet it is none of these
three things. There is no word for it in English; in Sanskrit it is
called *Vairagya*, an emotion, a feeling quite different from all
other ways of looking at life, an outlook which brings one into
an entirely different world of thought. The values of things and
conditions seem to change completely.

One might think that it would be an uninteresting life to be
indifferent, but that is not so; it is most interesting; it gives one
a feeling as if the burden of life was lightened. What a wonderful
feeling this is! Think what a little relaxation after a day's toil can
do, when one can just rest for a moment; what upliftment
comes, what soothing vibrations, and how the mind feels re-
freshed! If then the spirit has the same experience, feeling that
the load it is continually carrying day and night is lifted, then it
too feels widened for a moment. What a blessing this is! It cannot be spoken of in words, but the one who has had even a
slight experience of it can comprehend its value.

No doubt there comes a time in a man's life when even if he
were initiated a thousand times by nature he still seeks for a
guide walking on earth. Many will say, "Why is God not sufficient? Why must there be someone between God and man?
Why must it be a man who is just as limited as we are? Why can
we not reach the spirit of God directly?" But in a man who is

your enemy and who has tortured you throughout your life, in another who is your greatest friend, and in your teacher who inspires and guides you, in all these is to be seen the hand of God. They have all three guided you on the path of inspiration; they are all three needed in order that you may go further in life. The one who has disappointed you, who has harmed you, is also your initiator, for he has taught you something, he has put you on the road, even if not in the right way. And he who is your friend is your initiator too, for he gives you the evidence of truth, the sign of reality; only love can give you a proof that there is something living, something real. And then there is the inspiring teacher, be he a humble man, an illiterate person, or a meditative soul, a great teacher or a humble one, he is what you think him to be, as everyone is to us what we think them to be.

If it were not necessary that man should guide his fellow men, Jesus Christ would not have been placed among those fishermen who could not understand Him; and yet He proved to be their guidance. The presence on earth of personalities such as Buddha and all the other teachers—many of them not even known to humanity though they have done so much, but who always are and always will be under whatever name and in whatever guise they may work—gives guidance to individuals and to humanity. God never reaches so directly and so fully as when He reaches through His teachers. The best way for God to reach human beings is through a human being; not through an angel but through man who is subject to birth and death and to all the faults that everyone has.

The way of the teacher with his initiate is strange. The greater the teacher the stranger may be the way. The teacher may test and the teacher may give trials; and the attitude of the teacher can never be understood, for a real teacher never commits himself. Neither his yes nor his no can be understood, for their meaning will be symbolical and very subtle. Perhaps he will speak in parables, perhaps he will teach without teaching, perhaps he will teach more just by a glance than by speaking a hundred words. Perhaps the presence of the teacher is of greater blessing in the life of the pupil than a hundred books he has read. Neither the indifference nor the sympathy of the teacher may be taken for what they appear to be, for in both there is something else. The more one studies the personality of the teacher, the more puzzled one becomes. The teacher is the initiator of life, he is the example of the subtlety of the whole of life.

Some people affirm that they have been initiated by a teacher on the other side. Well, perhaps they have; but are they not then in two worlds, the teacher in one and the initiate in the other? The initiate neither belongs to the teacher's world, nor does the teacher belong to his. This surely gives one less trouble than having to regard the pleasure of a living being; it is easier to feel that one has someone at one's back who is always whispering in one's ear and who speaks to one in dream or vision. It is not wrong and in some cases it is even true; there are souls, there are teachers who have perhaps not given on earth what they had to give, what they had to impart to others. But that is not the normal process. If it were a normal process then all the teachings would have been sent from the other side, but neither Buddha nor Jesus Christ nor Muhammad gave their teachings from there.

Today the prevailing thought is that no man should guide his fellow men and that there is no virtue in such guidance. This thought is so widespread that it is preventing people from seeking guidance from someone who is facing the same struggles, the same troubles, and who has the same experiences as everyone else. They go on rejecting such a man, as Jesus Christ was rejected, and at the same time they are looking for someone on the other plane! Many societies and groups have puzzled their heads so much over this subject that they have deprived themselves of that living water which follows its natural course through the world of man.

The work of the teacher is most subtle. It is like that of a jeweller who has to melt the gold first in order to make an ornament out of it. It has first to be melted, but once it is melted, once it is not hard metal any more but has become liquid, then it can be made into a crown or a ring or an ornament; then one can make a beautiful thing out of it.

And after this there is a further step. When the pupil has received the initiations that the teacher has to give, then the teacher's task is over, and he sends him on. The teacher does not hold the pupil indefinitely; he has his part to perform during the journey on the path, but then comes the inner initiation. This comes to the disciple who has become meditative, whose interest has become keen, whose outlook has widened, who sees life differently, whose conscience has acquired the habit of reasoning, of expanding.

No doubt in this experience also there is always help to be had. As help comes on earth so in the unseen world too that help then comes. It is as if we were in the street in some kind of difficulty; naturally others would come up to see if they could be of any assistance. So as one goes further one attracts the sympathy of beings who are always busy helping humanity from all planes of existence. The sympathy of those who are close to the one who is travelling on the path is attracted, giving him a hand to go forward. It is that giving of a hand which is called initiation. There are so many different initiations: they are all steps by which to go upward.

In conclusion I shall mention what is attained through initiation. What one attains is that realization for which we are born, which is our life's purpose. Unless we approach life's purpose, nothing we do will help us sufficiently; it will only help us perhaps in a certain need of ours, but not any further. There is only one thing which gives complete satisfaction, and that is to arrive at self-realization. It is not simple and it needs more than just meditation and concentration, although these are of great help in the attainment of self-realization. And those who believe that by reading a book on Yoga they can get to that realization are mistaken. They are mistaken because it is a phenomenon; and it is by this phenomenon that one proceeds further.

Some people think that by straightforward study, by purely scientific study, they can come to realization, but in order to attain self-realization a certain way of life is necessary. Is it the life that religious people teach, that one should live in such and such a way? Is it a life according to certain principles, certain dogmas? No, nothing of that kind. It is the continual process of effacing the self; it is just like grinding something which is very hard; it is a continual grinding of the self. And the more that self is softened, the more highly a person evolves and the greater his personality becomes. No matter what power and inspiration a person may have acquired, if there is no self-effacement nothing is accomplished. The result brought about by initiation is self-effacement, and it is self-effacement which is needed in order to arrive at true wisdom.

VII

Discipleship

ONE WONDERS, ESPECIALLY in the Western part of the world, what the path of discipleship may really be. Although the path of discipleship was the path of those who followed Christ and all the other teachers, the modern trend of thought has taken away much of the ideal that existed in the past. It is not only that the ideal of discipleship seems to be little known, but even the ideal attitude towards motherhood and fatherhood, as well as toward the aged, seems to be less understood. This change in the ideal of the world has worked unwittingly to such an extent that world conflicts have been the result in our times. The troubles between nations and classes, in social and domestic life, all arise for one and the same reason. If someone were to ask me what is the cause of today's world unrest, I would answer that it is the lack of idealism.

In ancient times the path of discipleship was a lesson to be applied in every direction of life. Man is not only his body; he is his soul. When a child is born on earth, that is not the time that the soul is born; the soul is born from the moment that consideration is born. This birth of consideration is in reality the birth of the soul; man shows his soul in his consideration. Some become considerate as children, others perhaps do not awaken to consideration throughout their whole life. Love is called a divine element, but love's divine expression is nothing but consideration; and it would not be very wrong to say that love without consideration is not fully divine. Love that has no consideration loses its fragrance. Moreover intelligence is not consideration. It is the balance of love and intelligence, it is the action and reaction of love and intelligence upon each other that produce consideration. Children who are considerate are more precious than jewels to their parents. The man who is considerate, the friend who has consideration, all those with whom we come in contact who are considerate, we value most.

Thus it is the lesson of consideration given by the spiritual teachers which may be called the path of discipleship. This does not mean that the great teachers have wanted the discipleship, devotion, or respect of the pupils for themselves. If any teacher expects that, he cannot be a teacher. How could he then be a spiritual teacher, as he must be above all this in order to be above them? But respect, devotion, and consideration are taught for the disciple's own advantage, as an attribute that must be cultivated. Until now there has been a custom in India, which I myself experienced when young, that the first things the parents taught their children were respect for the teacher, consideration, and a kindly inclination. A modern child going to school has not the same idea. He thinks the teacher is appointed to perform a certain duty; he hardly knows the teacher nor does the teacher know him well. When he comes home he has the same tendency towards his parents as at school. Most children grow up thinking that all the attention their parents give them is only part of their duty; at most they will think, "Perhaps one day if I am able I shall repay it." The ancient idea was different. For instance the Prophet Muhammad taught his disciples that the greatest debt every man had to pay was to his mother, and if he wished his sins to be forgiven he must so act through life that at the end his mother before passing from this earth would say, "I have forgiven you the debt." There was nothing a man could give or do, neither money nor service, which would enable him to say, "I have paid my debt"; no, his mother must say, "I have forgiven you that debt." What does this teach? It teaches the value of that unselfish love which is above all earthly passion.

If we inquire of our self within for what purpose we have come on earth and why we have become human beings, wondering whether it would perhaps have been better to remain angels, the answer will certainly come to the wise, from his own heart, that we are here to experience a fuller life, to become fully human. For it is through being considerate that we become fully human. Every action done with consideration is valuable, every word said with consideration is precious. The whole teaching of Christ—"Blessed are the meek . . . the poor in spirit"—teaches one thing: consideration. Although it seems simple, yet it is a hard lesson to learn. The more we wish to act according to this ideal, the more we realize that we fail. The further we go on the path of consideration, the more delicate do the eyes of our perception become; we feel and regret the slightest mistake.

It is not every soul that takes the trouble to tread this path. Everyone is not a plant; there are many who are rocks, and these do not want to be considerate, they think it is too much trouble. Of course the stone has no pain, it is the one who feels who has pain. Still, it is in feeling that there is life; life's joy is so great that even with pain one would rather be a living being than a rock, for there is a joy in living, in feeling alive, which cannot be expressed in words. After how many millions of years has the life buried in stones and rocks risen to the human being! Even so if a person wishes to stay a rock, he had better stay so, though the natural inclination in every person should be to develop the human qualities fully.

The first lesson that the pupil learns on the path of discipleship is what is called *Yaqin* in Sufi terms, which means confidence. This confidence he first gives to the one whom he considers his teacher, his spiritual guide.

In the giving of confidence, three kinds of people can be distinguished. One gives a part of his confidence and cannot give another part. He is wobbling and thinking, "Yes, I believe I have confidence; perhaps I have, perhaps I have not." And this sort of confidence puts him in a very difficult position. It would be better not to have it at all. It is like lukewarm water, neither hot nor cold. In all things this person will do the same, in business, in his profession. He trusts and doubts, he trusts and fears. He is not walking in the sky, he is not walking on the earth; he is in between the two. Then there is another kind, the one who gives his confidence to the teacher, but he is not sure about himself, he is not inwardly sure if he has given it. This person has no confidence in himself, he is not sure of himself; therefore his confidence is of no value. And the third kind of person is the one who gives confidence because he feels confident. This confidence alone can rightfully be called Yaqin.

Jesus Christ had people of all these categories around him. Thousands of people of the first category came, thronged round the Master, then left him. It did not take one moment for them to be attracted, nor one moment for them to leave the Master.

In the second category are those who go on for some time, just as a drunken man goes on and on; but when they are sober again things become clear to them and they ask themselves, "Where am I going? Not in the right direction." Thousands and thousands in this category followed the masters and prophets, but those who stayed to the end of the test were those who before giving their confidence to the teacher first had confidence in their own heart. It is they who, if the earth turned to water and the water turned to earth, if the sky came down and the earth rose up, would remain unshaken, firm in the belief they have once gained. It is by discipleship that a person learns the moral that in whatever position he is, as husband or wife, son or daughter, servant or friend, he will follow with confidence, firm and steady wherever he goes.

After acquiring Yaqin there comes a test, and that is sacrifice. That is the ideal on the path of God. The most precious possession there is, is not too valuable, nothing is too great to sacrifice. Not one of the disciples of the Prophet—the real disciples— thought even their life too great a sacrifice if it was needed. The story of Ali is very well known: a plot was discovered, that one night some enemies wanted to kill the Prophet, and Ali learnt about it. He did not tell the Prophet, but persuaded him to leave home. He himself stayed, for he knew that if he went too the assassins would follow him and find out where the Prophet was. He slept in the same bed in place of the Prophet, so that the assassins might find him, though at the same time he did not intend to lose his life if he could fight them off. The consequence was that the plot failed and the enemies could not touch either the Prophet or Ali.

This is only one instance, but there are thousands of instances which show that the friendship formed in God and truth between the teacher and the disciple is for always, and that nothing in the world is able to break it. If the spiritual link cannot hold, how can a material link keep intact? It will wear out, being only a worldly link. If spiritual thought cannot form a link between two souls, what else can constitute such a strong tie that it can last both here and in the hereafter?

The third lesson on the path of discipleship is imitation; this means imitating the teacher in his every attitude, his attitude towards the friend, towards the enemy, towards the foolish, and towards the wise. If the pupil acts as he wishes and the teacher acts as he wishes, then there is no benefit, however great the sacrifice and devotion. No teaching or meditation is as great or valuable as the imitation of the teacher in the path of truth. In the imitation of the teacher the whole secret of the spiritual life is hidden. No doubt it is not only the imitation of his outward action, but also of his inner tendency.

The fourth lesson that the disciple learns is different again. This lesson is to turn the inward thought of the teacher outward, until he grows to see his teacher in everyone and everything, in the wise, in the foolish, and in all forms.

Finally, by the fifth lesson the disciple learns to give everything that he has so far given to his teacher—devotion, sacrifice, service, respect—to all, because he has learnt to see his teacher in all.

One person will perhaps learn nothing all his life, whereas another will learn all five lessons in a short time. There is a story of a person who went to a teacher and said to him, "I would like to be your pupil, your disciple." The teacher said, "Yes; I shall be very glad." This man, conscious of so many faults, was surprised that the teacher was willing to accept him as a disciple. He said, "But I wonder if you know how many faults I have?" The teacher said, "Yes, I already know your faults, yet I accept you as my pupil."—"But I have very bad faults," he said, "I am fond of gambling." The teacher said, "That does not matter much."—"I am inclined to drink sometimes," he said. The teacher said, "That does not matter much."—"Well," he said, "there are many other faults." The teacher said, "I do not mind.

But now that I have accepted all your faults, you must accept one condition from your teacher."—"Yes, most willingly," he said. "What is it?" The teacher said, "You may indulge in your faults, but not in my presence; only that much respect you must reserve for your teacher." The teacher knew that all five attributes of discipleship were natural to him, and he made him an initiate. And as soon as he went out and had an inclination to gamble or to drink he saw the face of his murshid before him. When after some time he returned to the teacher, the teacher smilingly asked, "Did you commit any faults?" He answered, "Oh no, the great difficulty is that whenever I want to commit any of my usual faults my murshid pursues me!"

Do not think that this spirit is only cultivated; this spirit may be found in an innocent child. When I once asked a little child of four years, "Have you been naughty?" it answered, "I would like to be naughty, but my goodness will not let me." This shows us that the spirit of discipleship is in us. But we should always remember that he who is a teacher is a disciple himself.

In reality there is no such thing as a teacher; God alone is Teacher, we are all disciples. The lesson we all have to learn is that of discipleship; it is the first and the last lesson.

VIII

Four Kinds of Discipleship

THERE ARE FOUR KINDS of disciples, of whom only one can be described as a real disciple. One kind is the disciple of modern times who comes and says to his teacher, "We will study this book together," or "Have you read that book? It is most interesting," or "I have learnt from someone else before, and now I would like to learn what I can from you and then I will pass on to something which is still more interesting." Such a person may be called a student, but not yet a disciple. His spirit is not that of a disciple; it is the spirit of a student who goes from one university, from one college, to another; from one professor he passes into the hands of another. He may be well suited for such intellectual pursuits, but the spirit of the disciple is different.

Then there is another type who thinks, "What I can get out of him I will get. And when I have collected it, then I shall use it in the way I think best." Well, his way is that of a thief who says, "I will take what I can from the purse of this person, and then I shall spend it for my own purpose." This is a wrong attitude, because spiritual inspiration and power cannot be stolen; a thief cannot take them; and if he has this attitude such a disciple may remain with a teacher for a hundred years and still leave empty-handed. There are many in this world today who make intellectual theft their occupation; anything intellectual they find, they take it and use it. But they do not know what harm they do by this attitude. They paralyse their minds and they close their own spirit.

Then there is a third wrong tendency of a disciple: to keep back something which is most essential, namely confidence. He will say, "Tell me all you can teach me, all I can learn, give me all that you have," but in his mind he says, "I will not give you my confidence, for I do not yet know if this road is right or wrong for me. When you have taught me I shall judge, then I shall see what it is. But until then I do not give you my confidence, though my ears are tuned to your words." This is the third wrong tendency. As long as a disciple will not give his confidence to his spiritual guide, he will not get the full benefit of his teaching.

The fourth kind is the right kind of discipleship. And this does not come by just thinking that one would like to go on the spiritual path, or that one would like to be a disciple, a mureed, a *chela,* but there comes a time in every person's life when circumstances have tried him so much that he begins to feel the wish to find a word of enlightenment, some counsel, some guidance, a direction on the path of truth. When the values of all things and beings are changing in his eyes, that is the time he begins to feel hungry for spiritual guidance. Bread is meant for the hungry, not for those who are quite satisfied. If a person like this goes in search of a teacher, he takes the right step; but there is a difficulty, and this is that if he wants to test the teacher first, then there is no end to the testing. He can go from one teacher to another, from the earthly being to the heavenly being, testing everyone, and in the end what will he find? Imperfection. He is looking for it, and he will find it. Man is an imperfect being, a human being, a limited being. If he wants to find perfection in a limited being, he will always end by being disappointed whoever he meets, whether it is an angel or a human being. If he were simple enough to accept any teacher that came his way and said, "I will be your mureed," it would be easier, though this is perhaps not always practicable.

Someone asked a Brahmin, "Why do you worship a god of rock, an idol of stone? Look, here I am, a worshipper of the God who is in heaven. This rock does not listen to you, it has no ears." And the Brahmin said, "If you have no faith, even the God in heaven will not hear you; and if you have faith this rock will have ears to hear."

The middle way and the best way is to consult one's own intuition and inspiration. If one's intuition says, "I will seek guidance from this teacher, whether he is raised high by the whole of humanity or whether he is looked at with contempt and prejudice by thousands, I do not care," then one follows the principle of constancy in adhering to that one teacher. But if a person is not constant on the spiritual path he will naturally have difficulty in the end. For what is constancy? Constancy is the reflection of eternity. And what is truth? Truth is eternity, and so in seeking for truth one must learn the principle of constancy.

The disciple has to have full confidence in the teacher's guidance, in the direction that is given to him by the teacher. The Buddhists who regard a spiritual teacher with great reverence say, "We do not care whether he is well-known or not; and even if he is we do not know if he will accept our reverence; and if he receives it we are not sure he needs it." Worship can only be given to those of whose presence we are conscious; and it is especially intended for the spiritual teacher, for he shows us the only path that frees us from all the pains of which this life is full. That is why among all other obligations involving earthly gain and benefit the obligation to the spiritual teacher is the greatest, for it is concerned with the liberation of the soul on its journey toward nirvana, which is the only desire of every soul.

The teacher does not always teach in plain words. The spiritual teacher has a thousand ways. It may be that by his prayers he can guide his disciple; it may be by his thought, his feeling, or his sympathy, so that even at a distance he may guide him. And therefore when a disciple thinks that he can be taught only by words or teachings, by practices or exercises, it is a great mistake.

In order to get the right disciples and the right people to come to him, a Sufi who lived in Hyderabad made a wonderful arrangement. He got a grumpy woman to sit just near his house; and to anyone who came to see the great teacher, she would say all kinds of things against the teacher: how unkind he was, how cruel, how neglectful, how lazy; there was nothing she would leave unsaid. And as a result out of a hundred, ninety-five would turn back; they would not dare to come near him. Perhaps only five would come, wanting to form their own opinion about him. And the teacher was very pleased that the ninety-five went away, for what they had come to find was not there; it was somewhere else.

There is another side to this question. The first thing the
teacher does is to find out what is the pressing need of his disciple. Certainly, the disciple has come to seek after truth and to
be guided to the path of God, but at the same time it is the
psychological task of the teacher to give his thought first to the
pressing need of his disciple, whether the disciple speaks of it or
not. And the teacher's effort is directed toward removing that
first difficulty, because he knows it to be an obstacle in the disciple's way. It is easy for a soul to tread the spiritual path because
it is the spiritual path that the soul is looking for. God is the
seeking of every soul, and every soul will make its way naturally,
providing there is nothing to obstruct it, and so the most pressing need is the removal of any obstruction. Thus a desire can be
fulfilled, it can be conquered, or it can be removed. If it is fulfilled so much the better. If it is not right to fulfil it then it
should be conquered or removed in order to clear the way. The
teacher never thinks that he is concerned with his disciple only
in his spiritual progress, in his attainment of God, for if there is
something blocking the way of the disciple it will not be easy
for the teacher to help him.

There are three faculties which the teacher considers essential to develop in the disciple: deepening the sympathy, showing
the way to harmony, and awakening the spirit of beauty. One
often sees that without being taught any particular formula, or
receiving any particular lesson on these three subjects, the soul
of a sincere disciple will grow under the guidance of the right
teacher like a plant which is carefully reared and watered every
day and every month and every year. And without knowing it
himself he will begin to show these three qualities, the ever-
growing sympathy, the harmonizing quality increasing every
day more and more, and the expression and understanding and
appreciation of beauty in all its forms.

One may ask, is there no going backward? Well, sometimes
there is a sensation of going backward; just as when one is at

sea, the ship may move in such a way that one sometimes has the feeling that one is going backward although one is really going forward; one can have the same sensation when riding on an elephant or a camel. When in the lives of some disciples this sensation is felt, it is nothing but a proof of life. Nevertheless a disciple will often feel that since he became a disciple he finds many more faults in himself than he had ever seen before. This may be so, but it does not mean that his faults have increased; it only means that now his eyes have become wider open so that every day he sees many more faults than before.

There is always a great danger on the spiritual path that the disciple has to overcome: he may develop a feeling of being exalted, of knowing more than other people, of being better than other people. As soon as a person thinks, "I am more," the doors of knowledge are closed. He will no more be able to widen his knowledge, because automatically the doors of his heart are closed the moment he says, "I know." Spiritual knowledge, the knowledge of life, is so intoxicating, so exalting, it gives such a great joy, that one begins to pour out one's knowledge before anyone who comes along as soon as this knowledge springs up. But if at that time the disciple could realize that he should conserve that kindling of the light, reserve it, keep it within himself, and let it deepen, then his words would not be necessary, his presence would enlighten people; but as soon as the spring rises, and he pours forth what comes out of that spring in words, although on the one side his vanity will be satisfied yet on the other his energy will be exhausted. The little spring that had risen he has poured out before others, and he remains without power. This is why reserve is taught to the true disciple, the conserving of inspiration and power. The one who speaks is not always wise; it is the one who listens who is wise.

During discipleship the first period may be called the period of observation; in this the disciple with a respectful attitude observes everything good and bad and right and wrong, without expressing any opinion about them. And every day this reveals to the disciple a new idea on the subject. Today he thinks it is wrong, but does not say so; tomorrow he wonders how it can be wrong. The day after tomorrow he thinks, "But can this really be wrong?" while on the fourth day he may think that it is not wrong, and on the fifth day that it is right. And he may follow the same process with what is right, if only he does not express himself on the first day. It is the foolish who always readily express their opinion; the wise keep it back. By keeping their opinion back they become wiser every day; by expressing their opinion they continually become less wise.

The second thing that is most important for the disciple is learning. And how is he to learn? Every word the disciple hears coming from the lips of the teacher is a whole sacred book. Instead of reading a sacred book of any religion from beginning to end, he has taken in one word of the teacher, and that is the same. By meditating upon it, by thinking about it, by pondering upon it, he makes that word a plant from which fruit and flowers come. A book is one thing and a living word is another. Perhaps a whole book could be written by the inspiration of one living word of the teacher. Besides the disciple practices all the meditations given to him, and by these exercises he develops within him that inspiration, that power which is meant to be developed in the disciple.

And the third step forward for the disciple lies in testing the inspiration, the power that he has received. One might ask, how can one test it? Life can give a thousand examples of every idea that one has thought about. If one has learnt from within that a certain idea is wrong or right, then life itself is an example which shows why it is wrong or why it is right.

If a person does not become enlightened, one can find the explanation by watching the rain: it falls upon all trees, but it is according to the response of those trees that they grow and bear fruit. The sun shines upon all the trees; it makes no distinction between them, but it is according to the response that the trees give to the sun that they profit by its sunshine. At the same time a mureed is very often an inspiration to the murshid. It is not the murshid who teaches; it is God who teaches. The murshid is only a medium, and as high as the response of the mureed reaches, so strongly does it attract the message of God.

The mureed can inspire, but he can also cease to inspire. If there is no response on his side or if there is antagonism or lack of interest, then the inspiration of the murshid is shut off; just like the clouds which cannot produce a shower when they are above the desert. The desert affects them, but when the same clouds are above the forest the trees attract them and the rain falls.

The attributes of the disciple are reserve, thoughtfulness, consideration, balance, and sincerity. Special care should be taken that during the time of discipleship one does not become a teacher, for very often a growing soul is so eager to become a teacher that before he has finished the period of discipleship he becomes impatient. It should be remembered that all the great teachers of humanity such as Jesus Christ, Buddha, Muhammad, and Zarathushtra, have been great pupils; they have learned from the innocent child, they have learned from everyone, from every person that came near them. They have learned from every situation and every condition of the world; they have understood and they have learned. It is the desire to learn continually that makes one a teacher, and not the desire to become a teacher. As soon as a person thinks, "I am something of a teacher," he has lost ground. For there is only one teacher: God alone is the Teacher, and all others are His pupils. We all learn from life what life teaches us; and the day when a soul begins to think that he has learned all he had to learn, and that now he is a teacher, he is very much mistaken. The greatest teachers of humanity have learned from humanity more than they have taught.

IX

The Attitude of a Disciple

A MUREED'S ATTITUDE TOWARD LIFE must be hopeful; towards his motives courageous; toward his murshid faithful; toward the cause sincere; toward that object which he has to accomplish earnest without the slightest doubt. In every aspect of life it is our attitude which counts and which in the end proves to be creative of all kinds of phenomena. Both success and failure depend upon it, as in the Hindu saying, "If the attitude is right, all will come right."

There is a natural tendency in the seeker on the spiritual path to wonder if he is really progressing. And very often he begins to wonder from the day he sets foot on the path. It is like asking "Shall I be able to digest?" while one is still eating. The spiritual path leads to selflessness. The more we worry about ourselves, the less progress we make, because our whole striving should be to forget the self; it is mostly the self which obstructs the path. The path is made for the soul, and it is natural and easy for the soul to find it. Therefore when a person is wondering about his progress he is wasting his time; it is like standing still on the path on which one must go forward.

Can anyone distinguish how his face and body change day by day? No, for one cannot point out distinct signs of change from one day to another; and if one cannot properly distinguish any change in the external self, then how can one expect to distinguish change in the inner process? It is not something that can be weighed on the scales as one weighs oneself on coming back from a holiday and sees that one has gained or lost several pounds. There is no such gain in spiritual progress.

Then there are some who imagine that they have progressed for a certain time but are then going backward. They are discouraged and say, "I thought I had arrived somewhere, but surely it must have been an illusion." But life is like the sea, and the sea is not always calm. There are times when the sea is rough and then the boat naturally moves up and down, and to think while the boat is moving downward that it will sink is a mistake. It is going down in order to go up; it is its movement; it is natural. A mureed is subject to such experiences in the path of life. Life will take its own course. The one who sails will have many times to meet a rough sea; he has to be prepared for this and not be frightened or discouraged. He still has to go on through life. If life's journey were soft and smooth there would be no need for spiritual development. He has to have control of the rudder to be able to go through both calm seas and storms.

Sometimes the mureed wonders what others are saying and if they are displeased or pleased; if they are displeased he thinks he is not progressing. But this has nothing to do with progress. Those who are displeased would be displeased even with Jesus Christ, and at the same time they might be pleased with the worst person. The displeasure of others does not mean that one is not progressing.

Then if conditions are adverse the murseed thinks that he is not on the right path. But does it mean that the ship is not on its right course if a storm meets it? Neither the murshid nor God is responsible if the conditions are adverse, and the best thing is to meet them, to be more brave and courageous and to make one's way through them. Ghazali, the great Sufi writer of Persia, says that spiritual progress is like shooting at a target in the dark. We do not know where the target is, we do not see it, but we shoot just the same.

The true ideal of the spiritual person is not great power nor a great amount of knowledge. His true ideal stands beyond power and knowledge; it is that which is limitless, incomprehensible, nameless, and formless. There are no milestones to count; one cannot say, "I have gone so many miles and there are so many still before me." This does not belong to a spiritual journey. The pursuit of the limitless is limitless, of the formless, formless; one cannot make it tangible. But then what is it that assures progress, what evidence have we to go on? There is only one evidence and that is our belief; there is one assurance and that is our faith. If we believe we can go on, if we are convinced we will, we must, reach our goal.

There are innumerable outer signs of one's progress, but one need not think in the absence of these signs that one is not progressing. What are these signs of progress? The first is that one feels inspiration, and that things which one could not understand yesterday are easy today. Yet if there are things which one is not ready to understand one should have patience till tomorrow. Agitating against lack of inspiration means closing the doors to inspiration. Agitation is not allowed on this path; agitation disturbs our rhythm and paralyses us, and then we prove in the end to be our own enemy. But people will generally not admit this and blame others instead; or if they have kind feelings toward others then they blame the circumstances, although very often it is their own lack of patience rather than other people or the conditions.

The next sign of progress is that one begins to feel power. To some extent it may manifest physically and also mentally; and later the power may manifest in one's affairs in life. As spiritual pursuit is endless, so power has no end.

The third sign of progress is that one begins to feel a joy, a happiness. But in spite of that feeling it is possible that clouds of depression and despair may come from without, and one might think at that moment that all the happiness and joy which one had gained spiritually was snatched away. But that is not so. If spiritual joy could be snatched away it would not be spiritual joy. It is not like material comforts; when these are taken away from us we have lost them; but spiritual joy is ours, it is our property; no death nor decay can take it away from us. Changing clouds like those which surround the sun might surround our joy, but when they are scattered we will find our property still there in our own heart. It is something we can depend upon, something nobody can take away from us.

There is another sign of progress, and that is that one becomes fearless. Whatever be the situation in life, nothing seems to frighten one any more, even death. Then one becomes fearless in all that might seem frightening, and a brave spirit develops, a spirit which gives one patience and strength to struggle against all adverse conditions however terrible they seem to be. It can even develop to such an extent that one would like to fight with death. To such a person nothing seems so horrible that he would feel helpless before it.

Still another sign of progress is that at times one begins to feel peaceful. This may increase so much that a restful feeling comes in the heart. One might be in solitude, but even if one is in a crowd one still feels restful. Life in the world is most exciting; it has a tiring effect upon a sensitive person. When one is restless the conditions in life can make one experience the greatest discomfort, for there is no greater pain than restlessness. And if there is any remedy for the lack of peace, it is spiritual progress. Once peace is developed in a soul, that soul feels such a great power and has such a great influence upon those who approach it and upon all upsetting conditions and jarring influences coming from all sides that just as water makes the dust settle down, so all jarring influences settle down under the feet of the peaceful. What do we learn from the story told in the Bible of Daniel who was thrown into the lions' den, what does this story suggest? Was it Daniel's hypnotism which calmed the lions? If it was hypnotism, let the hypnotizers of today go to the lions and try the experience! No, it was his inner peace. The influence of that peace acts so powerfully upon all passions that it even calms lions and makes them sleep.

One may make the excuse that one's surroundings are worrying one, that one's friends are troublesome or that one's enemies are horrible; but nothing can withstand that peace which is awakened in the heart. All must calm down, all must settle down like dust after water has been sprinkled on it.

But if this power does not come immediately to a mureed, let him not be disappointed. Can one expect this whole journey to be made in a week? I would not be surprised if many mureeds do expect this, but it is a lifelong journey and those who have really accomplished it are the ones who have never doubted that they would progress. They have never allowed this doubt to enter their minds to hinder them. They do not even concern themselves with this question. They only know that they must reach the goal, that they will reach it, and that if they do not reach it today they will reach it tomorrow. The right attitude is never to let one's mind feel, after one has taken some steps, that one must go to the right or to the left. If a man has that one strength which is faith, that is all the power he needs on the path. He can go forward and nothing will hinder him, and in the end he will accomplish his purpose.

THE PATH
OF THE MYSTIC

THERE ARE MYSTICS in all peoples, and there is a mystic side to all religions. This shows that mysticism does not come from the East or from the West; it is a human inheritance and belongs to the soul. Every religion—Buddhism, Christianity, Hinduism, Judaism, Islam—has a mystic aspect and this shows that mysticism belongs to every religion. It also shows that religion needs a mystical aspect to manifest in its fulness. In its last stages the world has passed through so much, so many centuries of materialism, that when nowadays one speaks of mysticism it is looked upon as something vague and incomprehensible.

Mysticism has always existed as a human inheritance, but the waves of materialism have effaced it. Sufis understand the difference between religion, morality, mysticism, and philosophy. Religion is a law of beauty given to humanity by the masters of life. Morality is a series of principles adopted by a number of persons at a given period. Philosophy is a series of names, forms, conditions, and circumstances which are known by logic and knowledge. Mysticism is a way that is incomprehensible to most people, because it is a way of getting to the center of life and things; the other ways take centuries to get into them.

The source where mystics get their knowledge from is the divine source, of which Christ says, "Seek ye first the Kingdom of God and all things shall be added unto you." The ordinary person cannot understand that by sitting down and closing the eyes he can get knowledge without learning from exterior sources, because all his life he has been used to do so. And so it is that no religious man or philosopher, however good and pure, can attain to the knowledge of the mystic, because the mystic's knowledge is the greatest of all, just as a man standing on a mountain sees more than he who stands at the bottom. Can a person who wants to see the moon see it by looking on the ground? The words of Christ, "Seek ye first the Kingdom of God," are simple and yet understood by so few. The Christ spirit is the mystic spirit. Mysticism has always existed, even

before Christ. Buddha, Krishna, Moses, Muhammad, all walked
the path of the mystic. Can you tell about Krishna going to an
academy to learn? Or of Christ, or any other teacher learning
from other sources? No, their knowledge came from the divine
source.

Of course it makes the materialist wonder what that source
can be, where all the knowledge of the world is accumulated.
There is a very interesting story about Firdausi, the great Persian
poet, who has written the *Shah Namah*. A Shah of Persia once
desired documents of the ancient history of Persia, which no
one could find. There was only this poet who offered to write
that history. Everyone wondered how it could be done, but he
said, "Wait and you will see." He went into solitude for ten
years and then came back to the court with his books, the *Shah
Namah*. As he was still linked with the current of his solitary
life, he was not quite himself, and when one of the knights who
was very critical asked where one could find that knowledge,
Firdausi called him and said, "Come, sit by me and close your
eyes and see." Then that skeptical man saw all the pictures of
the ancient past pass before his eyes.

One may say that if one is to become a mystic for the knowledge that mysticism gives, it is not worthwhile, for there is already so much knowledge in the world. But it is not only knowledge that the soul seeks. There are other things, and one of them
is the longing for a lasting happiness, which man never has.
Whatever his condition or occupation, there is always something to complain of. This means that the home of a fish is
water, and on earth, even on a tray, it is not happy. The real
home of man is the Spirit of God, and elsewhere he will never
be satisfied. Man cannot understand this because he gets a little
substitute called pleasure. Another thing is that this pleasure is
momentary, and he must always suffer to get it; there is always
pain attached to pleasure and one must pay a good price for it.
True happiness is never experienced by man, until he has

touched that happiness that lives in his own heart. If you ask me what that happiness is like, I will tell you that it is impossible to explain to someone who has never tasted sugar what sugar is like. So one cannot explain this happiness except to someone who has felt it. There is another thing that mystics experience: ecstasy, and this cannot be explained either to one who has not felt it.

As there are many people who profess to be mystics, the real mystic keeps his experience to himself. As now in the Western world these thoughts are coming to be known, many people make a profession of clairvoyance and spirit communication; these are a degeneration of real mysticism which is the greatest thing. In the East these things are under the protection of religion. Think what loss the world has to face when mysticism degenerates into these forms, becoming commercialized; think of the sacrilege. Ecstasy is a well of light and of love which rises from the depth of man's heart—so high that it washes away all worries and troubles of life.

On the condition of man's heart depends this divine light, as the condition of the sea depends on the cosmic light. The cosmic changes make the sea agitated or calm. In one's heart there are moments of calm so great that it changes the whole atmosphere, and moments when the forces rise in man and wash away all troubles and worldly things. A poet or a gifted musician feels the same, as if you ask me why, I will say that it is because he could not create beauty unless he were an instrument of the divine beauty which is the greatest Creator.

Of course a mystic who dives deep and makes his heart an instrument of the divine Being experiences a greater ecstasy. And as the sea responds to the cosmos more than the land, so the heart of the mystic responds to the divine light more than the heart of the average man. His heart is liquid and that of the average man as frozen snow. Where does this freezing come from, since snow is also water? It comes from the thought of "my father, my mother, my beloved, my friends," "mine" separate from "yours," whereas the first lesson of the mystic is "Thou art and not I." It is not only complete surrender to God, it is self-effacement. What does the symbol of the cross explain? That Thou art, not me; my hands are not for me, they are all Thine. The Hindu saying "Die before death" does not mean suicide; it means the death of the "I," the separate self.

It is an error of man to call his tent his home. It is not a home, it is a tent. The body also is a tent which is temporary. Man calls it "I," but it is not "I." The pleasures of life make him forget what it is in him that says "I." Think only of the helplessness, sickness, and death of the body. Man never thinks of it but acts as if he should live thousands of years on this earth. There is no condition, rank, or wealth that can secure man's life. What is it that makes him think he is something when really he is nothing? If he can only think of what is nothing, he will realize that what was, is, and shall be, is One Being, God. Living with God is immortality. The Bible from the beginning teaches us to look for immortality within ourselves.

Therefore the mystic's path is not one of study but of meditation. In Sanskrit this is called Yoga, which means connection, yoke; it is to connect oneself with the divine Spirit. What disconnects one is the realization of one's separate entity, and what connects one is the thought of God.

Sufis, as all other mystics in all ages, have had their schools of this inner cult, and it must be considered a privilege that East and West are coming closer together, that the poetry and music and philosophy of East and West are becoming known to each other. The happiness of humanity lies in the friendship and harmony between East and West. There are many ways of doing this, but there is none better than the thought of God, and love between men. It is the essential spirit and by this all can unite.

The message of Sufism has been given in many countries; all are welcome, because in the love and light of the path of God there is no distinction. No doubt the movement of the Sufis is working to bring about a better understanding between races and peoples, but its essential work is to open the inner eyes of man.

APHORISMS

Aphorisms

The principles of mysticism rise from the heart of man; they are learned by intuition and proved by reason.

Mysticism is an experience.
It cannot be studied.
It cannot be put into words.
Those who write explanations of it or talk about colors, spirits, experiences, are not true mystics.

A mystic's God is Reality.

Mysticism without devotion is like uncooked food, it can never be assimilated.

The essence of spirituality and mysticism is readiness to serve the person next to us.

The aim of the mystic is to stretch his range of consciousness as wide as possible, so that he may touch the highest pride and the deepest humility.
The only fall for a mystic is to fall beneath the level of his ideal.

To every question that arises in the heart of the mystic he finds the answer in the life before him.

The beauty which the knower knows and the lover appreciates, the mystic worships.

The Mystic's Prayer:
>   Give me, Oh God,
>   Deep thoughts
>   High dreams
>   Few words
>   Much silence
>   The narrow path
>   The wide outlook
>   The end in peace.
>
>   Amen

Also by Hazrat Inayat Khan

THE SUFI MESSAGE OF SPIRITUAL LIBERTY
    The Way of Illumination
    The Soul, Whence and Whither
    The Art of Personality
    Mental Purification and Healing
    Spiritual Liberty
    The Alchemy of Happiness
    In an Eastern Rosegarden
    Sufi Teachings: The Art of Being
    The Unity of Religious Ideals
    Sufi Mysticism
    Philosophy, Psychology, Mysticism
    The Divinity of the Human Soul
    Sacred Readings: The Gathas
    Sufi Teachings: The Smiling Forehead

Published by the International Headquarters of the Sufi Movement and East West Publications, London and The Hague. Distributed in the United States by Omega Press, New Lebanon, New York.

Requests for information about the International Sufi Movement founded by Hazrat Inayat Khan to be sent to:

    The General Secretariat of the Sufi Movement
    Anna Paulownastraat 78
    2518 BJ The Hague
    The Netherlands
    Telephone: 31 (0)70 346 1594
    Fax: 31 (0)70 361 4864

Internet address of Sufi Center Bookstore: http://guess.worldweb.net/sufi
E-mail address: jmccaig@worldweb.net